United States
Department of
Agriculture

Forest Service

Pacific Northwest
Research Station

General Technical
Report
PNW-GTR-818

September 2010

Analyzing Lichen Indicator Data in the Forest Inventory and Analysis Program

Susan Will-Wolf

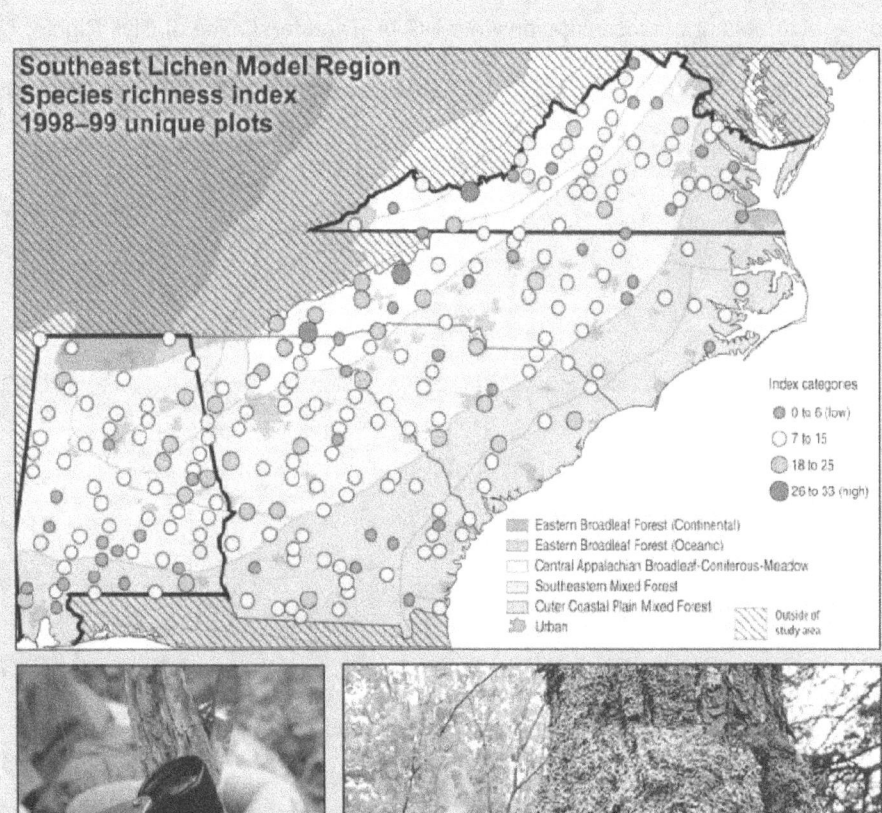

Southeast Lichen Model Region
Species richness index
1998–99 unique plots

Index categories
- 0 to 6 (low)
- 7 to 15
- 18 to 25
- 26 to 33 (high)

- Eastern Broadleaf Forest (Continental)
- Eastern Broadleaf Forest (Oceanic)
- Central Appalachian Broadleaf-Coniferous-Meadow
- Southeastern Mixed Forest
- Outer Coastal Plain Mixed Forest
- Urban
- Outside of study area

Author

Susan Will-Wolf is a research ecologist, Department of Botany, University of Wisconsin-Madison, 430 Lincoln Drive, Madison, WI 53706-1381 (Fax: 608-262-7509, Phone: 608-262-2754, E-mail: swwolf@wisc.edu).

This work was performed under cooperative agreements SRS 06-CA-11330145-079 and SRS 09-CA-11330145-101 with the Forest Inventory and Analysis program.

Cover

Map by Kandis Elliot. Photos: left, lichen training attendee examining lichens on bark with a hand lens, photo by Scott Bates; right, large common greenshield lichen (*Flavoparmelia caperata*) on trunk of sugar maple (*Acer saccharum*) tree, photo by Marie Trest.

Abstrat

Will-Wolf, Susan. 2010. Analyzing lichen indicator data in the Forest Inventory and Analysis Program. Gen. Tech. Rep. PNW-GTR-818. Portland, OR: U.S. Department of Agriculture, Forest Service, Pacific Northwest Research Station. 62 p.

Lichens are one of several forest health indicators sampled every year for a subset of plots on the permanent grid established by the Forest Inventory and Analysis (FIA) Program of the U.S. Department of Agriculture Forest Service. This report reviews analysis procedures for standard FIA lichen indicator data. Analyses of lichen data contribute to state, regional, and national reports that evaluate spatial pattern and temporal trends in forest biodiversity, air quality, and climate. Data collection and management follow standard national protocols. A lichen species richness index (the number of species per FIA plot) is available for all areas soon after data collection. Air quality and climate indexes (for defined regional gradients and based on lichen species composition at plots) are developed from an FIA lichen gradient model. Critical steps in standard data analysis include screening plots to exclude biased data, selection of appropriate populations, then analysis, presentation, and interpretation of data. Analysis of ranked indexes is recommended as the default data option, to compensate for frequent failure of indexes to meet assumptions for parametric statistical tests. Analysis of variance is the recommended default tool for standard analysis of both spatial pattern and trends across time. Because plot density is low, dot maps are currently recommended for display. Lichen data from the Southeast Lichen Model Region illustrate all steps in standard analysis. Lichen indicator data can also contribute to analyses of regional issues that may include specialized or experimental analysis techniques. Further development of analysis approaches is needed in several areas, including calibration between lichen gradient models for adjacent regions and better mapping techniques.

Keywords: Air quality, biodiversity, climate, environmental monitoring, forest health, lichens, pollution.

Summary

Lichens are one of several forest health indicators sampled every year for a subset of plots on the permanent grid established by the Forest Inventory and Analysis (FIA) Program of the U.S. Department of Agriculture Forest Service (USDA FS). Analyses of lichen data contribute to state, regional, and national reports that evaluate spatial pattern and temporal trends in forest biodiversity, air quality, and climate. This report reviews analysis procedures for standard FIA lichen indicator data and suggests guidelines for nonstandard analyses of FIA lichen indicator data.

Lichens have a long history as excellent biomonitors of nitrogen- and sulfur-based air pollutants; their response to climate is well-documented as well. Lichen community composition has been shown to be sensitive to air quality, climate, and other forest characteristics such as management history and fragmentation. Lichens have been part of national USDA FS monitoring programs since 1993; the monitoring protocol has remained the same throughout this history. After lichen sampling has begun in a region, gradient models are developed to generate indexes for lichen community response to important regional environmental factors. These response indexes are the most sensitive tools to evaluate forest health that are available from the lichen indicator. The main assessment questions addressed by the lichen indicator relate to air quality, climate, and biodiversity, but other questions are also being explored.

Data collection and management follow standard national protocols. Field samples are collected by trained nonspecialists. Field samples are identified by lichen specialists and the resulting data from the laboratory are the primary data used for analysis. A species richness index (the number of species per FIA plot) is available for all sampled areas. Air quality and climate indexes (defined for specific regions and based on lichen species abundance at plots) are available only after development and implementation of an FIA lichen gradient model.

A lichen species richness index and at least two lichen environmental response indexes are the typical plot-level attributes used for summary and analyses. Lichen data quality is evaluated by comparing crew field performance to an expert's field performance; this differs from other FIA indicators. Repeatability goals for lichen response indexes are set assuming the data quality objective has been met for the lichen species richness index. The lichen species richness index is the least sensitive of the available lichen indicators, but it is the most generally applicable across the United States. Lichen response indexes are more sensitive to patterns and change, but are currently applicable only within their own lichen model region.

This report focuses on all steps in recommended analyses of both kinds of lichen index; such analyses are suitable for inclusion in standard FIA reports. Plots should be screened before analysis, and plots that do not meet any of several criteria are considered for exclusion from analysis. Descriptive statistics and maps are useful population-level descriptive summaries for lichen indexes even without further analysis. Because plot density for all forest health indicators is low and appropriate populations for analysis cover large geographic areas, dot maps are currently recommended for display rather than maps showing continuous, smoothed values.

Statistical analysis of ranked lichen indexes is recommended as the default option, to compensate for frequent failure of data to meet assumptions for parametric statistical tests, and to free the analyst from the need to evaluate all relevant statistical properties of lichen indexes before analysis. Analysis of variance is the recommended default statistical tool for standard analysis of both spatial pattern and trends across time. Lichen data from the Southeast Lichen Model Region illustrate all steps in screening plots, selection of populations, analysis, presentation, and interpretation of results. Tables and figures present example standard core tables and maps that should be included in routine program reports.

Lichen indexes can also contribute to analyses focused on issues of regional interest that may include additional field sampling and specialized or experimental analysis techniques. Research should proceed on combining lichen indexes with other FIA variables for broad assessment of forest health and response to environmental factors such as air quality and climate. Further development of analysis tools to support standard analyses is needed in several areas, including calibration between lichen gradient models for adjacent regions and spatial interpolation of lichen index values for continuous mapping.

Contents

Tables

Figures

Introduction

The study of lichen communities in forest ecosystems allows assessment of several key questions concerning natural resource contamination, biodiversity, ability to provide ecosystem services, and sustainability of timber production. Lichens not only indicate the health of our forests, they also show a clearly established linkage to environmental stressors (fig. 1). Lichens are well known for their sensitivity to air quality. They respond to climate and to other factors affecting forests as well. The Forest Inventory and Analysis (FIA) Program of the U.S. Department of Agriculture Forest Service (USDA FS) surveys forests on permanent plots across the United States to inventory status and monitor trends over time. In this program, as is standard practice for most natural resource assessment, "inventory" refers to one-time assessment of the status of a resource, and "monitoring" refers to comparison between repeated inventories to evaluate changes in status and identify trends over time. A subset of FIA permanent plots is sampled every year for several forest health indicators (also referred to as phase 3 or P3 indicators) including the FIA lichen indicator. This program generates the most extensive lichen data set in the world. As such, it is an invaluable resource for exploring the relations of lichen communities to large-scale environmental factors and developing lichens as

Lichens are useful indicators of response to air pollution and climate.

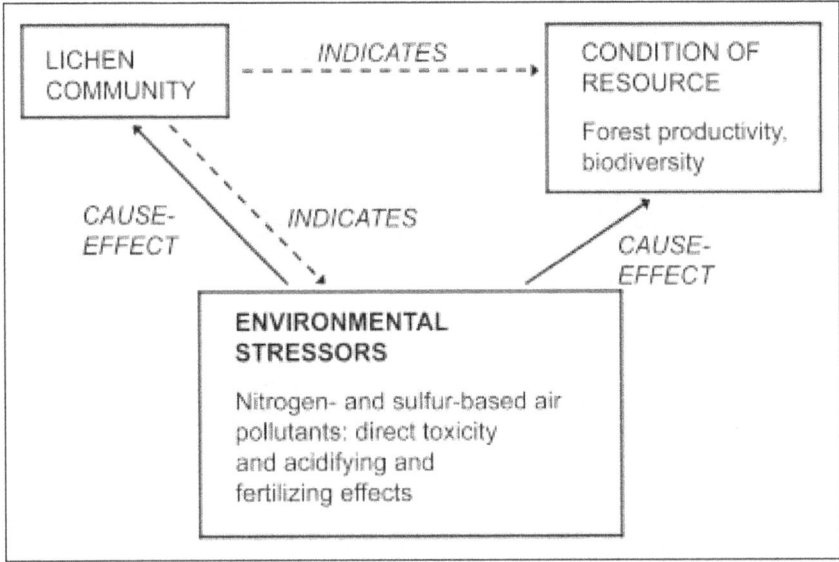

Figure 1—Conceptual model for the Forest Inventory and Analysis (FIA) Program lichen indicator. This diagram illustrates relations among air pollution as an example environmental stressor (or factor), the lichen community, and the entire forest ecosystem ("the resource"). A lichen indicator for a particular factor is interpreted based on scientific studies investigating cause-effect relations between that factor and response of lichens. Adapted from McCune et al. (1994).

indicators of forest response. A number of terms and formal phrases used repeatedly in this document are included in a glossary. Readers not familiar with the FIA Program or with the lichen indicator in the program might wish to read the glossary before reading this report.

The primary purpose of this report is to discuss appropriate analysis of FIA lichen data for standard reports. I review characteristics of the data, discuss issues that arise in data analysis, and present guidelines and recommended procedures for standard analyses of FIA lichen data. Many of these guidelines and procedures are applicable to other kinds of analyses, and some additional guidelines are presented for those pursuing nonstandard analyses of FIA lichen data. In this document, procedures are illustrated in text boxes with 1994–99 data from the Southeast (SE) Lichen Model Region (see glossary for definition of an FIA lichen model region) of the southern FIA region. Such a region is defined before analysis begins. This data set was selected because it includes many plots resampled several years apart; this is the most suitable lichen data set in the country to illustrate trend analysis.

This report includes five major sections:

- "Overview of the Lichen Indicator" presents the rationale for the indicator, literature review, and relevant program information.

- "Assessment Questions" reviews the most important questions addressed by the lichen indicator in the FIA Program.

- "Data Collection Protocols" summarizes standard procedures.

- "Analyzing and Presenting Standard Data" focuses on procedures for summarizing and analyzing data from the FIA lichen indicator. Statistical issues are reviewed in detail for nationally consistent analyses of standard plot data typically used in state, regional, and national reports (core products).

- "Guidelines for Additional and Future Analyses" outlines more specialized, more regional, or more experimental analyses, as well as topics in general analysis of indicator data that need further investigation.

Overview of the FIA Lichen Indicator

The current purpose of the FIA lichen indicator is to use lichen species and communities as biomonitors of changes in the air quality, climate, and biodiversity of forests. The lichen indicator is an important component of the FIA Program for several reasons: it assesses response to kinds of air pollution not monitored by other indicators; it gives signals of potential forest response to environmental factors independent from other forest health indicators; response signals are possibly clearer than for trees. Because lichens have little economic value, their response is not expected to be confounded as much by human management activities that affect tree response. The lichen indicator is also the only biological indicator in the FIA Program not based on vascular plants. It is thus an alternative to other indicators as a surrogate for the many nonrepresented members of forest communities (for instance birds, insects, mycorrhizal fungi). It is expected that other applications for the lichen indicator will be added as ongoing research supports their inclusion.

For the FIA Program, the lichen sample population is restricted to lichen species that can be distinguished in the field and identified in the laboratory in a timely manner. Field sampling protocol is designed to use standardized procedures appropriate for all forested sites that are cost-effective and sustainable for repeated sampling across the Nation. It is also designed to minimize the influence of local factors and within-plot variation; this enhances the efficiency of distinguishing responses to large-scale environmental factors over time and across large regions. Analysis of lichen data uses two kinds of lichen indexes. One is a primary index of biodiversity–the lichen species richness index for a plot. The other kind includes derived indexes (developed from models according to standardized protocols) of response to environmental factors. These latter are called lichen response indexes and are derived numbers that indicate relative response of lichens at a plot to an environmental factor (see "Glossary"). The term "lichen index" as used in this document refers to both kinds of index.

This section includes three subsections.

- "Background" reviews literature that supports the use of lichens as indicators of forest health and response to environment is reviewed.

- "Program History and Application" presents the history and development of the lichen indicator in the FIA Program.

- "Gradient Models" summarizes from other publications the development of gradient models to support use of the lichen indicator in the FIA program.

Background

A lichen is a close association (symbiosis) of a fungus with photosynthesizing algae and/or cyanobacteria. It looks and behaves ecologically like a single discrete organism. This organism-like association, the lichen "species," is named for the fungus even though it is clear that the biological characteristics of lichens cannot be understood merely from the fungus. A lichen community is an assemblage of these atypical "species" living together (Nash 2008).

Lichen species and communities have long histories as excellent indicators of air pollution, particularly long-term effects of acidic sulfur (S) and nitrogen (N) compounds (Hawksworth and Rose 1976, Smith et al. 1993, van Dobben 1993) resulting from industry, traffic, and urban centers. More recently, lichen communities have been shown to respond in different ways to ammonia and other usually alkaline N compounds that come primarily from agriculture and animal husbandry (Fenn et al. 2003; Jovan and McCune 2005, 2006; Sillett and Neitlich 1996; van Dobben and ter Braak 1998). Hundreds of papers worldwide (chronicled in the series "Literature on air pollution and lichens" in the journal *The Lichenologist*) and dozens of review papers and books (e.g., de Wit 1983, Nash and Wirth 1988, Nimis et al. 2002, Richardson 1988, Seaward 1993, Smith et al. 1993) continue to document the close relationship between lichen species, lichen communities, and air pollution.

Lichens have been found to give clearer response than vascular plants to N and S air pollution from a point source (Muir and McCune 1988) and to diffuse acidic deposition (Showman 1992). Much of the sensitivity of epiphytic lichens results from their weakly protective outer surfaces and reliance on atmospheric sources of nutrition (Nash 2008). Lichens provide a clear indication of S- and N-based air pollution effects directly upon lichens and indirectly upon their habitat.

Much literature also documents that forest lichen communities respond to primary climate variables such as precipitation and temperature, and to geographical gradients such as elevation and latitude that integrate climate factors (e.g., Bates and Farmer 1992; Dietrich and Scheidegger 1997; Nash 2008; Will-Wolf et al. 2002a, 2006). Lichen data from the FIA Program contribute to this literature by documenting the relations of forest lichen communities to environmental gradients across many geographic regions (McCune 2000). Studies of lichen response to changes in climate have increased in recent years (e.g., Arseneault and Payette 1992, Belnap and Lange 2005, Ellis et al. 2007, Søchting 2004). Other recent studies have shown that lichens are sensitive to landscape structure and land use context, and to forest management (review in Will-Wolf et al. 2002a). Counts of lichen species in fixed-area plots and lichen species composition at sites each have long histories in literature (e.g., reviews in Bates and Farmer 1992, Nimis et al. 2002) that support their use for summarizing the status and response of lichen communities with respect to large-scale environmental factors.

Program History and Application

The lichen indicator is one of several forest health (P3) indicators in the FIA Program. With this indicator, one can first assess the general condition of lichen communities in a region. Then over time, one can monitor change in composition, diversity, and response to major regional factors such as climate and air quality. The lichen indicator was developed in 1990-92 for the Environmental Monitoring and Assessment Program. It was part of the USDA FS Forest Health Monitoring (FHM) Program 1993-99, and starting in 2000 has been part of the FIA Program. The field and laboratory protocols for the lichen indicator have remained stable throughout its history. Data from the current inventory year are always fully backward compatible with data from the first lichen inventory year.

The lichen indicator is a powerful tool in FIA for assessing forest health.

In the design of a lichen bioindicator, both scientific validity and practical feasibility must be addressed (McCune 2000, Smith et al. 1993, Will-Wolf 1988, Will-Wolf et al. 2002b). The FIA lichen indicator protocol enables tracking of response to air pollution and other major environmental factors across regions in a scientifically valid and cost-effective manner (McCune et al. 1997a, 1997b; Will-Wolf et al. 2006). This comes at the expense of obtaining data too coarse for assessing response to within-plot variables such as lichen substrate or microhabitat and tree species composition (Dietrich and Scheidegger 1997, McCune 2000, Will-Wolf et al. 2004). Expertise with lichens is not a standard skill of people trained in forestry practices. Since the development of the lichen indicator and its use in the FHM and FIA Programs, a specialist trained in both lichenology and community ecology (currently titled the FIA lichen indicator advisor) has guided development and management of the lichen indicator.

The FIA lichen indicator is implemented in two phases (fig. 2). The calibration phase involves analysis of data from standard FIA plots and supplemental plots to develop a lichen gradient model. The lichen gradient model links lichen species composition in a predefined region to environmental factors of interest such as air quality and climate (subsection "Gradient Models" below). Until completion of the calibration phase, lichen species count for a plot (the lichen species richness index) is the primary index available. During the application phase, lichen data from standard FIA plots are used to calculate response indexes (numbers representing response to an environmental factor as defined by a lichen gradient model) for each FIA plot. These lichen response indexes are the strongest lichen indicators for monitoring status and trends over time in response to the defined environmental factors.

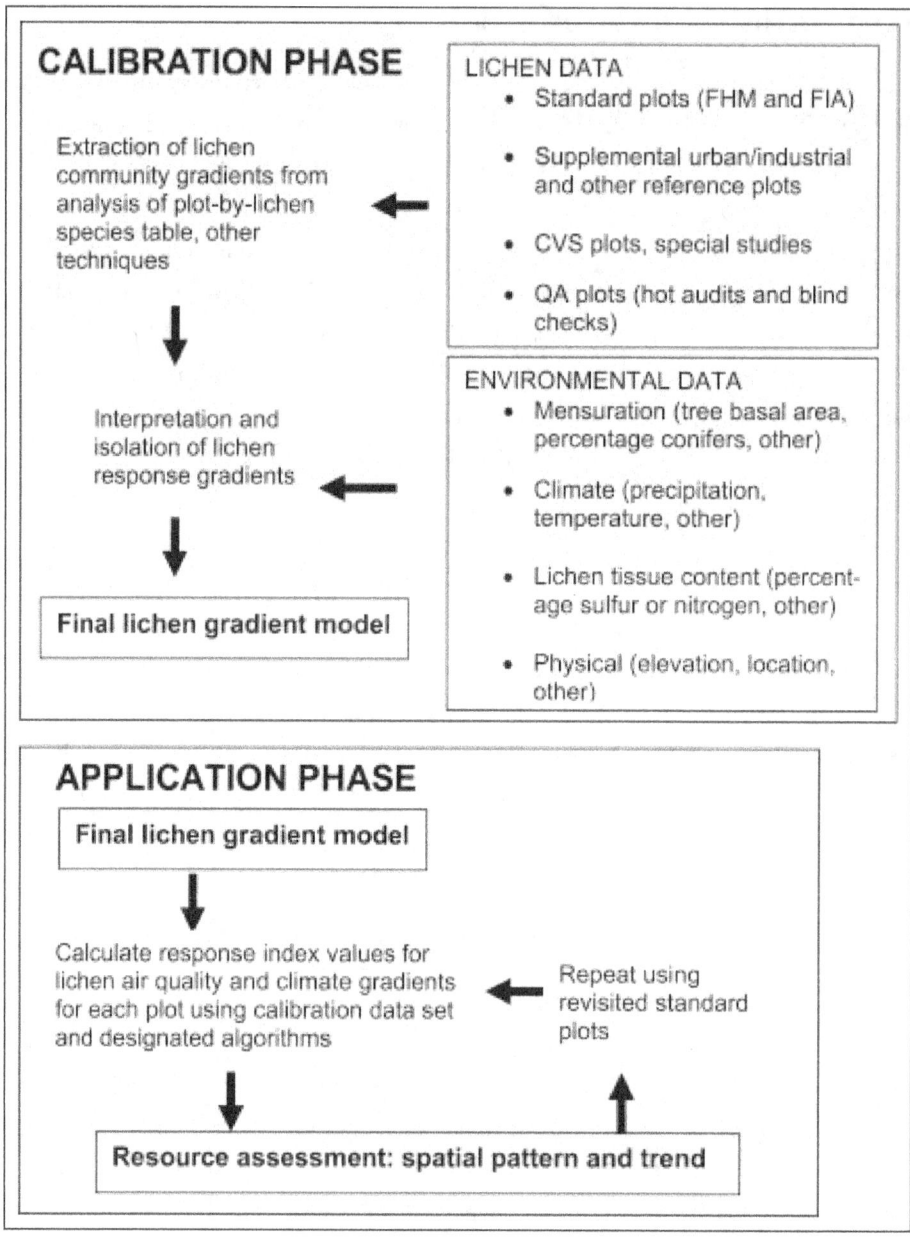

Figure 2—The two phases of implementation of the Forest Inventory and Analysis (FIA) Program lichen indicator. During the calibration phase, standard FIA plot data and other data are collected and a gradient model is developed. During the application phase, lichen response indexes are calculated for new plots from the gradient model based on data collected. These plot indexes are used to analyze patterns across space and trends over time related to the defined gradients. Other abbreviations: CVS = U.S. Department of Agriculture Forest Service National Forest current vegetation survey, FHM = Forest Health Monitoring Program, QA = quality assessment. Adapted from McCune et al. (1994).

Gradient Models

An "FIA lichen gradient model" is developed for a particular predefined geographic region, an "FIA lichen model region," using standard analytical techniques including multivariate community data analysis, regression analysis, and indicator species analysis (Legendre and Legendre 1998, McCune and Grace 2002). The two phrases in quotes above have very specific meanings in the FIA Program (see "Glossary") that are explained below. These phrases are used in the same sense without quotes throughout this report. Models are developed by experts in lichenology and community ecology, usually through contracts with the FIA Program. Goals, rationale, guidelines, and standardized requirements for developing a lichen gradient model are presented in detail in Will-Wolf and Neitlich (2010), and are summarized here. Progress in developing models is listed in table 1 for 18 of 21 proposed forested regions of the United States as outlined in figure 3. These models have been funded at the rate of about one every 2 years during 1993–2009.

Table 1—Forest Inventory and Analysis (FIA) Program lichen model regions and progress toward completion of models

Lichen Model Region	Progress	Publication
New England	In progress	
Mid Atlantic	In progress	
Southeast	Completed	McCune et al. 1997a, 1997b
North Central	In future	
Ohio Valley	In future	
South Central	In future	
Northern Rockies	In future	
Middle and Southern Rockies (Colorado)	Completed	McCune et al. 1998
Southwest	In future	
Pacific Northwest West	Completed	Geiser and Neitlich 2007
Pacific Northwest East/Northern Great Basin	In progress	
Greater Central Valley (of California)	Completed	Jovan and McCune 2004, 2005
California Sierras	Completed	Jovan and McCune 2004, 2006
Central Great Basin	In future	
Alaska–Southeast/South Central	Funded	
Alaska–Southwest/South Central	In future	
Alaska–Interior and Arctic	In future	
Hawaii	In future	

Note: Twenty-one lichen model regions have been identified as of 2010. Three regions on figure 3—South Florida, Northwestern California, and Southern California Coast—are not listed in this table. Their small size probably precludes use of standard FIA lichen gradient model development techniques; indexes of lichen response to environmental drivers of interest will be developed in other ways.

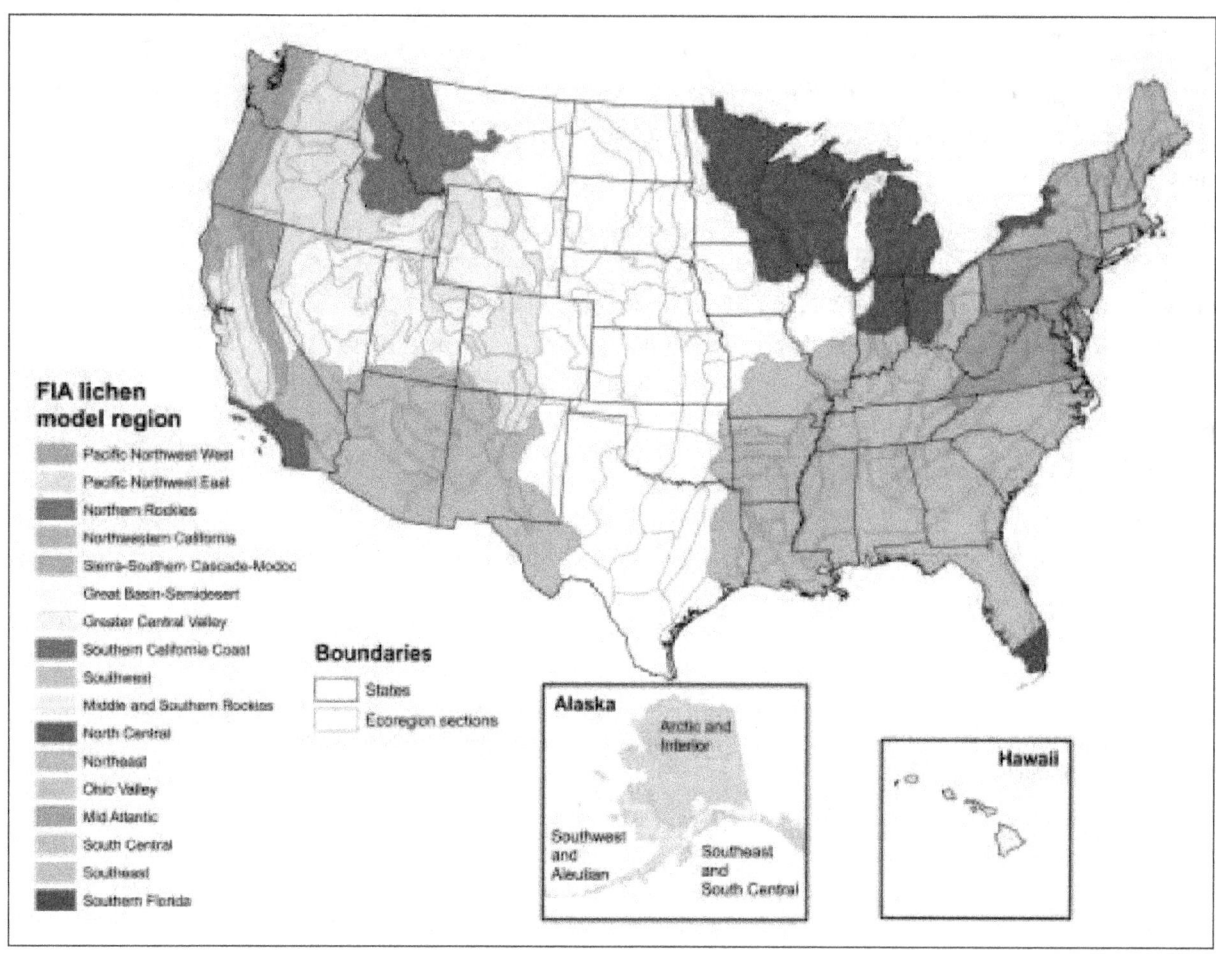

FIA lichen
model region

Pacific Northwest West
Pacific Northwest East
Northern Rockies
Northwestern California
Sierra-Southern-Cascade-Modoc
Great Basin-Semidesert
Greater Central Valley
Southern California Coast
Southwest
Middle and Southern Rockies
North Central
Northeast
Ohio Valley
Mid Atlantic
South Central
Southeast
Southern Florida

Boundaries

States
Ecoregion sections

Alaska

Arctic and Interior

Southwest and Aleutian

Southeast and South Central

Hawaii

Figure 3—Boundaries of existing and proposed Forest Inventory and Analysis (FIA) Program lichen model regions. Twenty-one regions (including Alaska and Hawaii) have been outlined as of 2010. Lichen model regions with completed models (see table 1) have had boundaries tested and found to be ecologically supported. Those with models in development or not yet begun have tentative boundaries that may change as a lichen gradient model is completed. Many boundaries follow Bailey et al. (1994). From Will-Wolf and Neitlich (in press).

The goal for each lichen gradient model is to link lichen species composition of a plot to single derived numbers (response indexes) representing the plot's relation to important environmental factors such as air quality and climate. Each lichen response gradient defined for a model must be statistically independent of all other lichen response gradients defined for that particular model. Developers demonstrate that response indexes for lichen gradients are independent of local factors such as stand age, total tree basal area, and percentage of basal area in conifers or hardwoods (Geiser and Neitlich 2007; Jovan and McCune 2005, 2006; McCune et al. 1997b). Each model includes procedures for estimating goodness-of-fit of a plot to a model.

Boundaries of an official FIA lichen model region are decided before the development of an FIA lichen gradient model for that region (fig. 3). A lichen model region usually includes several Bailey's Ecoregion Provinces (Bailey et al. 1994, Cleland et al. 2005) and several states, often does not end at state boundaries, and may cross FIA administrative region boundaries. Each FIA forest health plot (P3 plot) is assigned to a particular lichen model region as boundaries are defined. Final boundaries of such a region may be adjusted during development of a model for that region through an iterative process, so boundaries and even number of regions as presented in figure 3 may well change. Once a lichen gradient model has been developed, all plots for that region with lichen data are assigned lichen response indexes for all defined gradients following instructions for that model. Alteration of boundaries and reassignment of plots to different regions may also be done after repeated comparison of lichen gradient models for adjacent regions. Standards for repeatability of lichen response indexes established from the model are the basis for estimating the precision of pattern and trend estimation. The lichen response indexes are archived and are the primary basis for analysis of patterns and trends. Interpretation of these indexes is specific to each lichen model region.

Assessment Questions

Three major categories of assessment questions applicable to the lichen indicator, "Air Quality," "Climate," and "Biodiversity," (each discussed in separate subsections below) have been identified so far. "Other Categories of Assessment Questions," are outlined in a fourth subsection.

Air Quality

Does regional air quality affect our forests? Have the effects changed? If so, is air quality improving or deteriorating? In what areas is it changing?

Sulfur and nitrogen air pollutants are stressors that clearly affect lichen communities, even when effects on higher plants are difficult to detect. Lichen communities may be used to indicate air quality and identify where effects of these pollutants on other components of the forest ecosystem are more likely to be found (Jovan 2009). Bioindicators have many advantages over physical monitoring (e.g., NADP 2010, NAPAP 1991): they are cheaper and require no maintenance, they can provide data for any field site, and they reflect response of indicators rather than merely the presence of pollutants. Bioindicator response is specific to the conditions at a particular field site, as compared with the general and imprecise predictions generated from modeled or extrapolated pollution values (Nimis et al. 2002).

Climate

Are changes in climate affecting our forests? If so, how do we characterize the effects? In what areas is it changing?

Changing climate is an ever-more-likely prospect whose impact on forests needs to be assessed. Changes in climate will also likely interact with other factors to affect forests indirectly in unexpected ways. The lichen indicator has some distinct advantages over other FIA indicators to assess potential for effects of climate change on forests. A lichen climate index is a routine product of development of a gradient model; tracking climate response is thus by design a standard outcome from analysis of lichen data. For other FIA indicators, researchers are in the early stages of developing new specific climate-response indexes from field protocols not originally developed with this in mind. The lichen indicator focuses on large-scale response, whereas most other indicators also reflect much within-plot variation. These advantages of lichen climate indexes hold even though the magnitude of response by lichens to climate may well be similar to responses of other forest components such as understory vegetation or tree species.

Biodiversity

Is the lichen component of biodiversity changing through time? What environmental drivers seem to be most strongly linked to patterns and changes in lichen biodiversity?

Lichens contribute a substantial proportion of the visible species of many forests. For example, similar numbers of macrolichen species and vascular plant species are found in *Abies grandis* forests in western Montana (Lesica et al. 1991). In a typical southeastern forest, 20 to 60 lichen species are recorded in a single FIA plot sample (McCune et al. 1997b). Lichens play numerous functional roles in temperate forest ecosystems (Nash 2008), including significant N-fixation and nutrient cycling (Pike 1978) and serving as forage for mammals and arthropods (Dawson et al. 1987; Maser et al. 1985, 1986; Rominger and Oldemeyer 1989; Servheen and Lyon 1989; Sharnoff and Rosentreter 2008).

The FIA lichen species richness index tracks one aspect of diversity patterns. Because both air pollution and climate change have potential to affect long-term sustainability and biodiversity, lichen response indexes for these factors give insights into the causes of patterns and trends of lichen biodiversity. Comparisons of patterns from lichen indexes with those from other forest components help identify general patterns of forest biodiversity and potential for change.

Other Categories of Assessment Questions

Other questions applicable to the lichen indicator are expected to arise in the future. For example, one category of questions currently being investigated concerns the effect of nearby land use on forests. Explicitly spatial variables representing various aspects of the landscape context of a plot are currently being developed in the FIA Program. The lichen indicator may be especially useful for tracking response to some of these spatial variables as well, as it is designed to minimize response to within-plot factors.

Data Collection Protocols

In contrast to most other FIA indicators, the primary lichen data come indirectly from field crews via the laboratory and office. Standardization and quality maintenance for laboratory and office activities are thus just as important as those for field sampling to maintain high quality of field data. The standardized "field sampling protocol" and "laboratory and office protocols" are summarized in separate subsections below.

Field Sampling Protocol

The FIA field sampling protocol is documented extensively in a manual regularly updated and now posted online (USDA FS 2004, 2010b); it is summarized here. This field protocol was developed specifically for large-scale forest monitoring in the United States (McCune 2000, McCune et al. 1997b). Tradeoffs in design of sample protocols for lichens must be accepted to achieve project goals efficiently (McCune 2000; McCune and Grace 2002; Will-Wolf 1988; Will-Wolf et al. 2002b, 2004). Lichen data are collected on the forest health (P3) subset of the full phase 2 (P2) FIA national grid. Forest health (P3) plot density is one forest health plot per about 39,072 ha (96,000 ac), 1/16 of full grid (P2) plot density (USDA FS 2010b). The lichen sample population is restricted to macrolichens (leafy or tufted lichens removable from their substrate) that can be distinguished in the field, can be collected easily, and can be identified in the laboratory in a timely manner.

Lichen data sampling protocols foster economical assessment of large-scale patterns.

The goal of the field sampling protocol is to find as many macrolichen species as possible within the guidelines. Lichen data are collected on an almost-circular plot (henceforth the FIA lichen plot or just "lichen plot") interspersed with but **not overlapping** the area of the four small subplots. The lichen plot is the gray area in figure 4; note it **does** overlap the area of the large macroplots. Trained and certified non-lichenologist FIA field crew members (one per crew) conduct a time-constrained (up to 2 hours) search of all standing natural woody substrates above 0.5 m (1.6 ft). Such substrates are typically found at any forested site. Field crew collect a sample of each lichen species and assign an abundance code according to the scale below. The lichen species abundance code is semiquantitative, supporting estimation of relative abundance of lichen species on a plot, but not estimation of absolute abundance nor of a quantitative correlation between lichen abundance and substrate abundance (from USDA FS 2010b). National standards for training and data quality assessment (QA) have been established (Will-Wolf 2007, Will-Wolf and Neitlich 2007) to help maintain consistent and high data quality from field sampling.

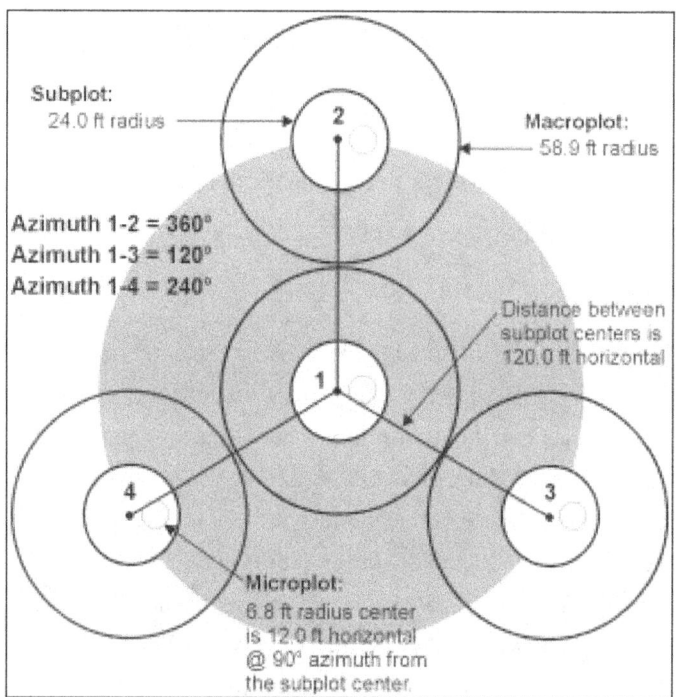

Figure 4—The standard Forest Inventory and Analysis (FIA) Program lichen field plot. The lichen sampling plot is the gray area on this diagram. Data for other FIA indicators are mostly collected from the four subplots. From USDA FS (2010b).

Lichen species abundance code and interpretation:

Code	Abundance
1	Rare (1 to 3 separate individual lichens in lichen plot)
2	Uncommon (4 to 10 individuals in lichen plot)
3	Common (>10 individuals in lichen plot but fewer than half of the boles and branches have that species present)
4	Abundant (more than half of all legal substrates in plot have the subject species present) Note: this code is not frequently assigned, but is valid. Make sure that more than one out of every two legal substrates (boles, branches, twigs, shrubs combined) host this species.

The properly labeled set of lichen samples from the plot constitutes the primary lichen field data for the plot. Secondary data about the lichen plot and lichen sampling conditions are recorded on a portable data recorder (PDR). These secondary data provide qualitative information that can aid lichen specialists and data analysts to evaluate anomalous observations. Plot samples are mailed to a lichen identification specialist who assigns species names to them.

Laboratory and Office Protocols

Laboratory and office data management includes three major tasks, each summarized in its own subsection: "Sample identification and data recording," "Data entry," and "Assigning response indexes."

Standardized procedures for each task help ensure high quality of final data. The first two tasks are summarized from a "Lichen Specialist Procedures" manual (Will-Wolf 2009). That manual also outlines qualifications needed for each task; the lichen indicator advisor works with FIA region staff to ensure only qualified personnel perform these tasks. Instructions for calculating lichen response indexes are included in the final report for each gradient model.

Sample identification and data recording—

Lichen identification specialists identify all lichen samples in each set of plot specimens received, using current identification aids. They follow established guidelines to standardize identification and usage of species names in the FIA Program. Taxonomic treatment of lichen species is documented in a master lichen species table and a lichen species comments table. Each is updated yearly, archived in program databases, and later posted as a reference table on the FIA data Web site

(USDA FS 2010a). Current reference tables are nationally consistent and fully backward compatible to 1993, the first lichen inventory year.

Specialists compute final abundance scores for each species on a plot from field scores following a standard protocol (McCune et al. 1997b, Will-Wolf 2009). Hardcopy lichen lists for each plot are archived with the indicator advisor and with the FIA region. Taxonomic decisions by lichen specialists are reviewed by the indicator advisor or representatives, and questions or uncertainties are resolved before final data submission for that year. A subset of plot samples including at least one sample of every lichen species identified by each specialist for each region are labeled with public plot information, properly curated, and deposited in public herbaria. These voucher sets are permanent public reference collections that document the expertise of specialists and lichen taxonomic decisions in the FIA Program.

Data entry—

Data are entered, usually by lichen identification specialists, following detailed instructions in the specialist procedures manual (Will-Wolf 2009, example in appendix). Data entry files list lichen species by codes that are permanently archived and posted in the master lichen species reference table on the FIA data Web site (USDA FS 2010a).

All data entry files are 100 percent proofread in the FIA lichen indicator advisor's office or by designated representatives who are qualified lichen specialists. They are then compiled into regionwide data files submitted to FIA regions in the winter/spring following each field season for uploading to the FIA database. Any upload errors are fully resolved by consultation between the indicator advisor and FIA information management representatives. The FIA database entries are the final error-checked products of the lichen data collection stream.

Each lichen data record is associated with a particular field season year, called an inventory year in the FIA Program (FIA database variable INVYR). Although lichen samples are routinely collected during a standard summer field season, other collection dates including the winter of the following year are possible. Archived data are stored and summarized based on the data record's inventory year, not the calendar year in which field data were collected (FIA database variable MEASYR). Updates to the reference lichen master species and reference lichen species taxonomic usage comment tables for the previous field season's lichen data are also labeled with the inventory year. Lichen data for a particular plot should always be

> **Laboratory and office protocols are critical to maintenance of FIA lichen data quality.**

associated for analysis with the plot's inventory year (variable INVYR), not with the plot's measurement year (variable MEASYR), if the two differ.

Assigning response indexes—

When a completed FIA lichen gradient model is in place, all plots sampled in that FIA lichen model region can be assigned indexes representing response to environmental factors as defined for that region. This should be done using final error-checked data from the FIA database. Such response indexes can be calculated only for plots that have lichen species recorded and have at least one species shared with the gradient model data set. Calculation of response indexes is based on abundances of the species found, not just on their presence at a plot.

Calculation of these response indexes has so far been performed by developers of the gradient model or by the indicator advisor. This task is being streamlined so it can be performed routinely by a regional FIA analyst with minimal consultation from the lichen indicator advisor. Response indexes are derived once for each plot and year and remain valid as long as the gradient model remains valid. The response indexes are currently available from FIA regions or from the indicator advisor. In the future, response indexes for plots will be uploaded to the FIA database as soon as they are calculated from the lichen laboratory data for each year, and will subsequently be posted on the FIA data Web site.

Response indexes are calculated for new plots following detailed instructions in an FIA lichen gradient model final report. The first step in the process is to identify and remove plots that do not meet criteria (such as a minimum tree basal area [BA]) established for accurate fitting to the model. The next step is to consult the current REF_LICHEN_SPECIES_COMMENTS table posted on the Web (USDA FS 2010a) and gradient model directions to reconcile taxonomic usage for each plot's inventory year with the gradient model inventory year. Data are modified accordingly before response indexes are calculated for plots. All instructions and all necessary data sets, equations, and other information are archived in each FIA administrative region for which the model applies. Strict adherence to the documented procedures for the applicable gradient model is required to ensure that the derived response indexes meet the quality criteria established from the model. A plot cannot be assigned a response index if no lichens were found when the plot was searched, or if none of the species found were included in the gradient model.

For a set of Southeast Model Region 1994–99 plots, the current REF_
LICHEN_SPECIES_COMMENTS table posted on the Web (USDA FS
2010a) was consulted about changes in taxonomic usage for lichen species
included in the data set. For those species, no changes were found for 1994
through 1999 or between the plot data set to be analyzed and the lichen
gradient model data set. So no species names and codes needed to be modified
before combining multiple years for analysis and for calculating lichen
response indexes for plots. Some plots could not be assigned a lichen response
index because no lichens were found there.

Quantitative criteria for adequate fit of a plot to a lichen gradient model are
established as part of model development (see subsection "Gradient Models" p. 7).
A plot whose fit value is outside a criterion is flagged as having poor fit to the
model. Flags for poor fit are to be archived in data tables along with the lichen
response indexes. Criteria for poor fit are to be defined and explained in archived
reference tables. A plot that fails to meet the fit criteria established for the model
should be considered for exclusion from data analysis.

Over long timespans (possibly up to 50 years), lichen community composition
of a region or its relation to environmental factors may shift such that an established lichen gradient model needs to be modified or replaced. The proportion of
plots for a lichen model region with flags for poor fit should be tracked over time.
A pattern of increase over several years in proportion of plots that fail to meet
criteria for adequate fit to the model is a signal that the model should be reevalu-
ated. Criteria for taking action will be developed as repeated sampling provides
data to support such decisions.

Analyzing and Presenting Standard Data

The emphasis in this document is on appropriate ways to apply robust and well-
studied methods to support nationally consistent analysis of standard FIA lichen
data. Choice of methods takes into account that lichen indicator data are collected
at quite low density (see section "Field Sampling Protocol" p. 11). For this report,
basic descriptive statistics are grouped with maps as descriptive summaries, and
more complicated numerical and statistical procedures are described as analyses.
Basic standard procedures for analyzing both point-in-time patterns and trends over

time are evaluated in detail. Example analyses were performed in SPSS[1] 2007 v16.01 or Microsoft Excel 2003 v. 11.8231.8221 SP3. Many of the guidelines are also applicable to a wide variety of additional analysis procedures; these are mentioned as appropriate. Experimental or very recently described techniques are not recommended for standard FIA data analysis; they are more appropriate for specific research projects. Examples of each procedure for the Southeast Lichen Model Region are described in text boxes and illustrated in tables 2 through 4 and figures 5 and 6.

This important section of the report includes four subsections:

- "Plot-Level Attributes" describes and evaluates plot-level indexes used for standard FIA analyses.

- "Population-Level Attributes" discusses selection of the population to study, screening of plots, and choice of attributes. Presentation of descriptive statistics and other summaries for population is valuable even without further analysis.

- "Recommended Population-Level Analyses" describes and evaluates procedures recommended for standard analyses applicable in general to all indexes derived from FIA lichen data.

- "Core Tables and Maps" outlines a minimum set of descriptive summaries and standard analyses for routine FIA reports.

Plot-Level Attributes

Plot-level attributes are the basic lichen community indicator information used for descriptive summaries and analyses. The list of lichen species found at a plot and their abundances are the plot-level data used to derive all plot attributes for lichens. It is not possible to partition data into subsections of the lichen plot analogous to subplots (fig. 4). Nor is it possible to associate lichen indicator data with particular species of trees even if only one species of live tree is recorded on subplots. Lichen samples may have come from any natural woody substrate including shrubs and dead snags.

 This section has three subsections explaining the two kinds of plot-level attributes currently defined and explaining quality evaluation for lichen data and indexes. "Lichen species richness index" is available for any FIA plot surveyed for lichens, and it can be compared for any/all FIA plots across the country.

Plot-level lichen indexes are the basic data used for analysis.

[1] The use of trade or firm names in this publication is for reader information and does not imply endorsement by the U.S. Department of Agriculture of any product or service.

Table 2—Forest Inventory and Analysis (FIA) Program lichen indicator example summary table: lichen species richness index, Southeast Lichen Model Region (SE), 1998–99

Parameter	SE Region 1998–99	Alabama[a] 1998–99	Virginia[a] 1998–99
Number of plots surveyed	257	64	53
Number of plots by richness index category[b c]			
0–6 species	61	15	15
7–15 species	159	41	34
16–25 species	34	8	3
>25 species	3	0	1
Median of richness index	10	10	8
Range of richness index (low to high)	0–33	2–22	0–27
Average of richness index (alpha diversity)	10.4	10.23	8.85
Standard deviation of richness index	5.32	4.77	5.28
Regional composition change (beta diversity)[d]	18.17	9.87	11.30
Total number of species found (gamma diversity)	189	101	100

Notes: Lichen species richness index is summarized for unique standard plots from Alabama, Virginia, and the entire SE region (includes also Georgia, North Carolina, and South Carolina) in the 1998 and 1999 inventory years. For Virginia, average lichen species richness index appears lower and relatively more plots are in lower richness index categories than for the region as a whole, whereas for Alabama both are similar to the region. Standard deviation and regional composition change are higher for the entire region than for either state, indicating greater differences in factors affecting lichen species richness than for Alabama or Virginia alone. Correlations with other plot vegetation and environmental factors would be needed to support statements about causes for variation in lichen species richness index. More than half the lichen species found in the five-state region are found in Alabama or Virginia, possibly because the samples included many widespread species. From nonparametric tests and analysis of variance (ANOVA) on ranked data for Alabama and Virginia, there are no significant differences in average rank of richness index between the two states, the two years, between years for states, and no state-by-year interaction effect (quantitative results not included).

[a] Indexes for Alabama and Virginia were compared using Mann-Whitney U and Kolmogorov-Smirnov Z tests, and ANOVA on ranked data.

[b] Categories are based on a cumulative distribution function of plot species richness for the SE gradient model (McCune et al. 1997b).

[c] Plots with no lichens found **are** included. Of 115 plots surveyed in 1998, 95 are included here; 3 were excluded for low tree basal area (BA); 17 resampled in 1999 were excluded. Of 179 plots surveyed in 1999, 162 are included here; 9 were excluded for low tree BA; 8 also sampled in 1998 were excluded. 95 + 162 = 257 plots.

[d] Regional species change (beta diversity) is calculated as total number of species found in the region (gamma diversity) divided by average plot species richness (alpha diversity).

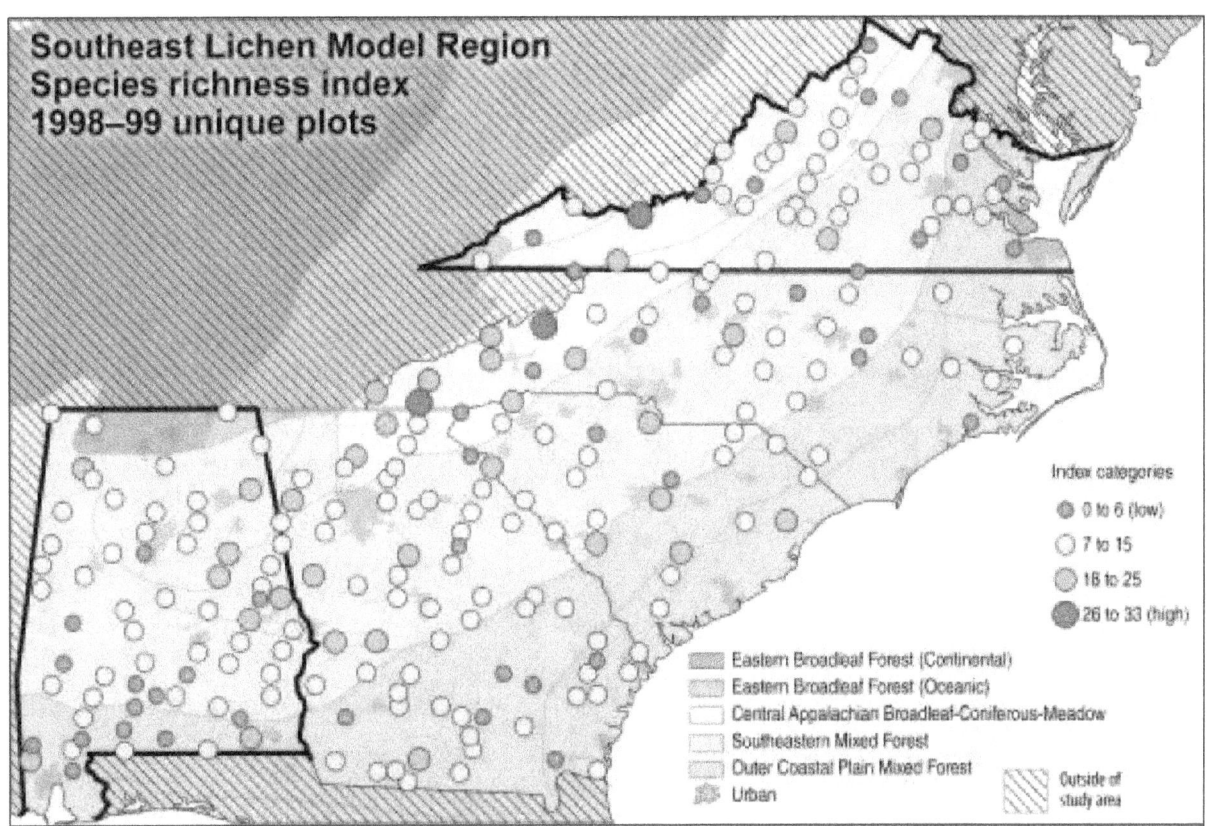

Figure 5—Forest Inventory and Analysis (FIA) Program lichen indicator example summary map: lichen species richness index plus ecoregion provinces for the Southeast Lichen Model Region, 1998–99. Plots with higher index values (higher number of species; orange and red dots) are more frequent in the Central Appalachian ecoregion province (at higher elevations) (Bailey et al. 1994). No strong distribution pattern of plots with the lowest index values (green dots) appears either by state or by ecoregion province. This map is an example of how FIA lichen indicator data for one or a group of years can be displayed. Virginia and Alabama are outlined as examples of how a state (or ecoregion) can be highlighted for a report focused on that unit. It is recommended that data for such a particular geographic unit be displayed as here, in the context of the larger lichen model region, for comparison purposes. If a lichen gradient model has been developed for the region, lichen air quality and climate indexes can be displayed similarly. Dot locations are not exact plot locations. Map by Kandis Elliot

> The lichen species richness index across the entire Southeast Lichen Model
> Region for 1998–99 is compared with Alabama and Virginia in example table
> 2. Plots in the species richness categories described in table 2 are mapped
> in example figure 5, with Alabama and Virginia outlined to emphasize their
> comparison with the rest of the region as might be done for a state report.
> Trends in lichen species richness index from 1994 to 1998 for the same region
> are summarized in table 4.

Table 3—Forest Inventory and Analysis (FIA) Program lichen indicator example summary table: lichen air quality index, Southeast Lichen Model Region (SE), 1998–99

Parameter	SE Region 1998–99	Alabama[a] 1998–99	Virginia[a] 1998–99
Number of plots surveyed	238	64	51
Number of plots by air quality index category[b c]			
Lowest (poorest air): index < 40	91	31	24
Intermediate: index 40–80	105	25	26
Highest (best air): index > 80	43	8	1
Median air quality index	49.23	44.10	43.81
Range of air quality index (low to high)	-9.22 to 113.48	-1.09 to 110.57	-9.22 to 113.48
Average of air quality index	50.73	45.80	39.88
Standard deviation of air quality index	26.88	26.12	21.71

Notes: Lichen air quality index is summarized for unique standard plots for Alabama, Virginia, and the entire SE region (includes also Georgia, North Carolina, South Carolina) in the 1998 and 1999 inventory years. The lichen air quality index is calculated from a model that relates lichen species composition to air quality independent of response to climate/environment (McCune et al. 1997b). For the current version of this model, a high air quality index suggests relatively cleaner air (**not** the convention recommended in text for lichen air quality indexes developed from future lichen gradient models). Virginia has a lower average index and a smaller proportion of plots in higher index categories when compared with the entire model region, indicating this state has lichen communities characteristic of relatively poorer air quality than the region as a whole. In contrast, Alabama is more similar to the entire region. Interestingly, the lowest and highest lichen air quality indexes are from Virginia and standard deviation of Virginia indexes is similar to the entire model region, indicating that it has lichen communities characteristic of the full range in air quality found for the whole region. From nonparametric statistical tests and analysis of variance (ANOVA) on ranked data for Alabama and Virginia, there is no significant difference in average rank of lichen air quality index between the two states, the two years, between years for states, and no state-by-year interaction effect (quantitative results not included).

[a] Indexes for Alabama and Virginia were compared using Mann-Whitney U and Kolmogorov-Smirnov Z tests, and ANOVA on ranked data.

[b] Categories are based on a cumulative distribution function of plot species richness for the SE Gradient Model (McCune et al. 1997b).

[c] Plots with no lichens are **excluded**, as are plots with poor fit to the SE Lichen Gradient Model. Of 95 plots from 1998 in table 2, 88 are included here; 2 had no lichen species; 5 had flags for poor fit. Of 162 plots from 1999 in table 2, 150 are included here; 2 had no lichen species; 10 had flags for poor fit. 88 + 150 = 238 plots. All Alabama plots from table 2 are included; two Virginia plots are excluded from this table.

"Lichen response indexes" are derived from models, are available only when a lichen gradient model is completed, and can be compared only for the same environmental factor in the same model region. "Quality assessment of plot-level indexes" describes in detail the designated quality goals and their evaluation for lichen indexes. Procedures for the lichen indicator differ from other FIA indicators. Summed plot-level abundance alone as an indicator, without reference to species composition, is not defined as a stand-alone lichen index in the FIA Program.

The currently recommended estimator of change for any of these indexes for a particular plot is simple subtraction of the index value for one year from that for another year. It is recommended that these change estimates always use the earlier(est) year as the base, with values for a later year subtracted from those for the base year. Applying a consistent convention to calculate change fosters more accurate interpretation by data analysts and by users of the reports and other products. Discussion of how to present and interpret change estimates is included in each subsection.

Lichen species richness index—

This is the number of species found in one sample from an FIA lichen plot. It is the simplest and most universal of the lichen plot-level attributes. A plot searched with no lichens found has a lichen species richness index of zero—an important data point. The index represents a biased subset (macrolichens only, timed survey) of all lichen species present on the plot. So it is better referred to as an index rather than "species richness" or "species diversity" without qualifiers.

For several reasons, lichen species richness index should be treated as a unitless ordinal number. It should **not** be considered as a valid estimate of number of lichen species per area, even though the index is the number of species found on a plot and the plot has a specified area. These reasons are:

1. Above a possible regionally defined minimum amount of available appropriate substrate (estimated by whole-plot live tree basal area [BA], for instance), lichen species richness index is usually not correlated with amount of substrate. Amount of substrate is itself expected to be independent of plot area.

2. Time-constrained samples are best considered to be biased subsamples of the set of all species in an area (Green 1979, Peckarsky 1984). The nature of this bias for FIA lichen data has not been described quantitatively, nor are there

Table 4—Forest Inventory and Analysis (FIA) Program lichen indicator example trend analysis: Southeast Lichen Model Region (SE), 1994 and 1998 paired plots

Lichen index	Average trend, 1994 minus 1998 (69 plots)	Average deviation, absolute values (69 plots)	Deviation <15 percent of gradient length (69 plots)	Wilcoxon Signed Ranks test, years (df=1)	Friedman's text, years (df=1)	Two-way ANOVA without replication, ranked data		Kruskal-Wallis test, plots (df=68)
						Years (df=1)	Plots (df=68)	
Species richness index[a]	2.754	5.391	—	Z = -3.304 p = 0.001**	T = 5.388 p = 0.020	F = 13.198 p = 0.001**	F = 2.258 p < 0.000**	H = 86.161 p = 0.068
Climate index[b]	3.178	17.829	43% of plots	Z = -1.696 p = 0.090	T = 0.941 p = 0.332	F = 1.243 p = 0.269	F = 3.731 p < 0.000**	H = 107.629 p = 0.002**
Air quality index[c]	12.184	23.688	41% of plots	Z = -3.1599 p = 0.002**	T = 9.058 p = 0.003*	F = 11.372 p = 0.001**	F = 2.308 p < 0.000**	H = 3.160 p = 0.033

Notes: Trends for lichen species richness index, lichen climate index, and lichen air quality index were evaluated for lichen data from standard plots sampled in 1994 and again in 1998, from Alabama, Georgia, and Virginia in the SE model region of the Southern FIA region. Only 69 plots had valid lichen response indexes for both years, even though 88 plots were sampled in each year. Analysis of variance (ANOVA) on ranked data and nonparametric tests (Wilcoxon, Friedman's, and Kruskal-Wallis) were performed. The positive value of average trend for all three indexes indicates declines in each index over time; 1998 values are subtracted from 1994 values. Average trend and deviation are convenient summaries of original data for characterizing patterns, but all tests used ranked data for calculations. For example, tests indicate a significant difference between ranks of lichen species richness index from 1994 to 1998, but no test reports the significance of differences in original lichen species richness index values. Multiple tests were performed on this data set, so to account for experiment-wide error, a probability of <0.02 is interpreted as significant and of <0.003 is interpreted as highly significant, denoted by * or ** respectively.

Rank of lichen species richness index declined significantly (fewer species) and lichen air quality index ranks are significantly lower (poorer air quality) in 1998 compared to 1994 values. Recall (table 3) that for the current SE model, a high value for the lichen air quality index suggests relatively cleaner air (**not** the convention recommended for the future). These results could together be interpreted as suggesting lichens have declined over time and declining air quality is a likely cause, but more factors need to be considered (see text box, p. 41). The nonsignificant results for lichen climate index suggest that lichen community response to climate has not changed during the 4-year timespan. As expected, lichen species richness, climate, and air quality indexes differ across plots from ANOVA, related to within-region variation in climate and air quality. Note that for variation across plots, the weaker Kruskal-Wallis test gives a significant result only for the lichen climate index, although results are close to significant for the other two indexes. For lichen species richness index between years, the weaker Friedman's test gives a borderline probability not marked as significant. Lichen species richness and air quality indexes each differed significantly across plots from only one test, although results from the other test are close to significant in each case.

[a] Decline in species richness index from 1994 to 1998 (significant trend).
[b] Decline in climate index from 1994 to 1998; plots became warmer over time (not a significant trend).
[c] Decline in air quality index from 1994 to 1998; air quality declined over time (significant trend).

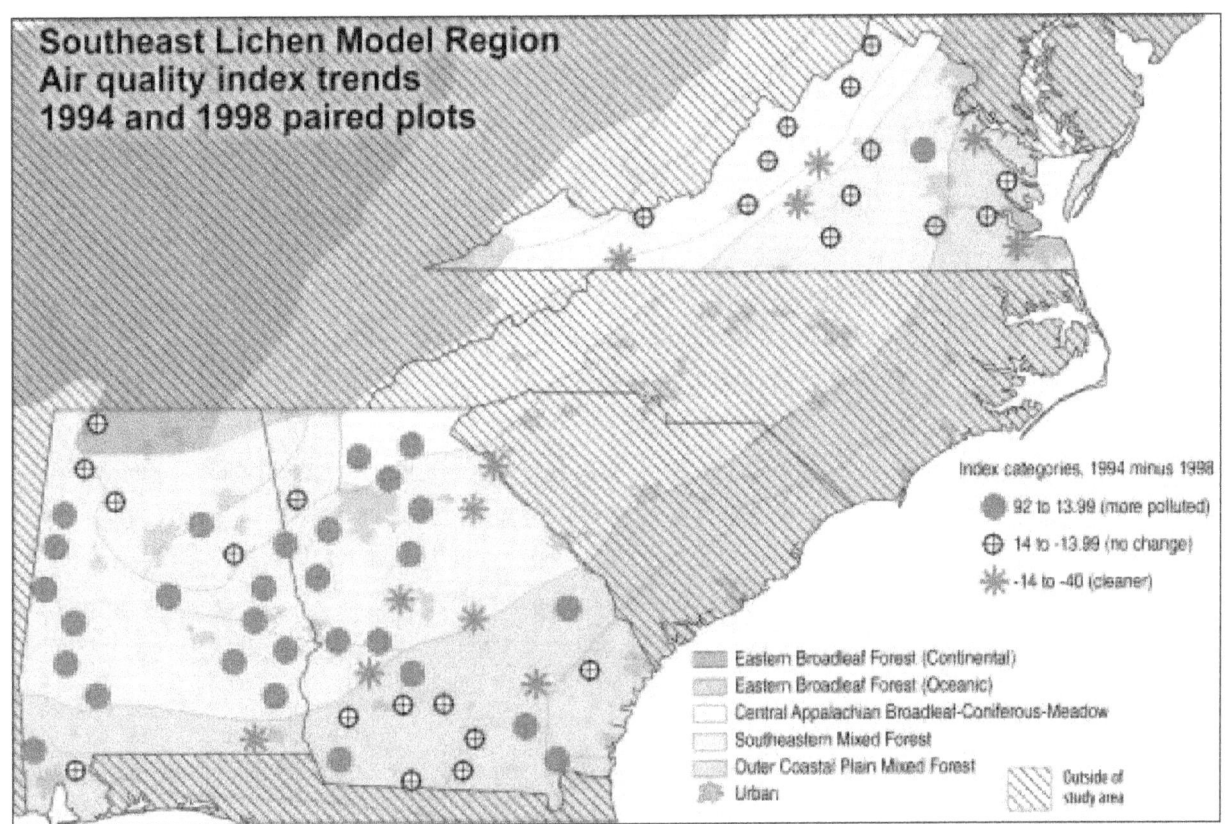

Figure 6—Forest Inventory and Analysis (FIA) Program lichen indicator example summary map: trends in lichen air quality index plus ecoregion provinces for Alabama, Georgia, and Virginia, 1994 to 1998. Lichen air quality indexes decreased significantly from 1994 to 1998 for the three-state area (see table 4), suggesting air quality declined. Recall (table 3) that for the current Southeast Lichen Gradient Model, a high value for the lichen air quality index suggests relatively cleaner air (**not** the recommended convention for future models). Most of the plots with decreases (red dots) apparently occurred in Alabama and Georgia, with only one Virginia plot showing decrease. Many of the plots with strong decreases are located relatively far from urban areas, and they are interspersed with plots showing no change (gray crosses) or strong increases (blue starbursts). Even with significant decreases in lichen air quality index from 1994 to 1998, Alabama and Georgia (the latter not shown in table 3) plots still have many plots with high lichen air quality index values in 1998–99, whereas Virginia has only one plot in the cleanest air quality category in 1998–99 (see table 3). The lack of strong spatial clustering of the red "decrease" dots within states suggests an analyst should further investigate before concluding an interpretation is justified that lichen air quality index trends indicate decreased air quality (see text box p. 41). This map is an example of how FIA lichen indicator trend data for repeated samples can be displayed. Dot locations are not exact plot locations. Map by Kandis Elliot.

Example lichen species richness index patterns are illustrated for the FIA Southeast Lichen Model Region with a 1998-99 summary in table 2 and a map in figure 5. For the same region and inventory years, example lichen response index patterns are summarized in table 3. Example trend analysis for the same region from 1994 to 1998 is presented in table 4, with a map in figure 6. Continuous index values have been divided into categories for mapping.

any plans to do so. One probable bias in FIA lichen data is that with time-constrained search, smaller macrolichen species are detected with less efficiency than larger macrolichens. Also, often up to two-thirds of all lichens on a plot are **not** macrolichens (Dietrich and Scheidegger 1997).

3. In studies using the FIA lichen protocol in a wide range of habitats (moist to dry, species-rich to relatively species-poor) across the United States, the highest species richness index for a single sample (usually from an expert) ranged from <50 percent to ~75 percent of the combined species count from multiple samples for the same plot (McCune et al. 1997a; Will-Wolf unpublished FIA lichen training data).

4. Species count routinely increases nonlinearly with increasing area (and by extension with increasing time). Rates of increase differ between regions and habitats (Palmer and White 1994, Peet 1974, Pielou 1975).

This index should not be summed with counts for other kinds of species (such as understory vegetation) as an overall biodiversity estimate for a whole plot. Other FIA species counts come from the four subplots (different summed area, fig. 4) and from much less time-constrained protocols.

The lichen species richness index can nevertheless be interpreted as an indicator of general forest health for trend monitoring and as an ordinal indicator of relative lichen species diversity at a plot (Green 1979, Smith et al. 1993, Will-Wolf 1988). The interpretation of the lichen species richness index is relatively straightforward–a higher number indicates more lichen species and higher lichen biodiversity. Lichen species richness index is often difficult to link with particular causal agents. In many areas it is correlated with both air quality and climate variables. The index is also sensitive to field crew performance, and it has high variability (see "Quality assessment of plot-level indexes" p. 27). So species richness index alone is considered a relatively imprecise estimator of forest health. Using only count of species for this index rather than their identity is at the same time the limitation that makes it an imprecise attribute and the advantage that makes this index comparable across all FIA plots in the United States.

The recommended convention for estimating change over time, simple subtraction from an earlier year, means that an increase in richness index from an earlier to a later year always yields a change estimate with a negative sign. This is not as counterintuitive as it may seem, as increase in species count does not always support an interpretation that forest conditions are improving. Higher species count may reflect increases in common species and mask loss of less common species characteristic of particular habitats.

Lichen species richness index is available soon after sampling and can be analyzed nationwide.

Lichen response indexes—

Two or more lichen response indexes–at least one air quality index and at least one climate index–are calculated for plots in an FIA lichen model region that has a model completed. Lichen gradient models developed to date have identified two to three important gradients in a region. Variation in a lichen response index is the strongest indicator of regional pattern, and change in response index of resampled plots is the strongest indicator of a trend over time.

Lichen response indexes are truly unitless numbers comparable only to other unitless numbers derived using the same model and procedure. The range of values for an environmental factor associated with a range of lichen response index values is reported with publication of a lichen gradient model. A lichen response index is calculated from the particular lichen species composition (including abundance) at a plot, rather than just a count of species. Thus it is applicable only within its own lichen model region, and it cannot be compared directly with lichen response indexes for a similar environmental factor (such as air quality) for plots in a different lichen model region. During calculation of lichen response indexes, each plot is evaluated for fit to the gradient model. A plot whose lichen response index is flagged as a "poor fit" based on an established fit criterion should be considered for exclusion from further analyses for that environmental factor.

In contrast to the lichen species richness index, the designation of meaning for a high value of a lichen response index can reasonably be linked to either the high or low end of a range of values for the associated environmental factor. The analyst should always be explicit in reports when interpreting the plot values for the lichen response index (e.g., "High values of this index suggest lower air quality.") or the estimate of change (e.g., "An increase in the value of this index over time means the climate appears to have become cooler.") for the related environmental factor (refer to lichen gradient model documentation). For most (but not all) published FIA lichen gradient models, the air quality index is constructed to assign a higher index value for plots with poorer air quality (suggesting more risk); this convention is recommended for all future models. Following this as well as the recommended convention for estimating change (lichen index for a later year is subtracted from the index for an earlier, "baseline" year), a negative value for **change** in lichen air quality index (increasing index over time) would thus indicate decline in air quality and higher suggested risk to forest health. In contrast, an index for a climate factor identifies a relationship without value attached (warmer is different from cooler, but not necessarily better or worse), and no standard for ordering a climate index is recommended. Interpretation of a climate index change estimate must be made relative to the values on the original lichen climate response gradient.

Lichen response indexes require a model for their calculation and are valid only within their model region.

For the Southeast Lichen Gradient Model, higher values of the lichen air quality index indicate cleaner air, and higher values of the lichen climate index indicate cooler conditions. Note air quality index values for this first model published do **not** follow the convention recommended in this document. In example table 3, the lichen air quality index for the entire Southeast Lichen Model Region as compared with Alabama and Virginia is interpreted in the body of the table. The rationale for the index categories is explained in a footnote. For estimating change in this region (table 4), the value of an index in 1998 is subtracted from its value for that plot in 1994. Changes in lichen air quality and climate indexes are interpreted in footnotes. In figure 6, the mapped change in lichen air quality index is interpreted in the caption.

Quality assessment of plot-level indexes—

Repeatability of lichen response indexes based on the lichen sample protocol (USDA FS 2004, 2010b) is assessed assuming the lichen species richness index met quality objectives. Unlike other FIA indicators (Pollard and Palmer 1998), the field measurement quality objective (MQO) for lichen species richness index is based on achieving a minimum standard of 65 percent of the lichen specialist's species count, not on repeatability of field crew performance (Patterson et al., in press). Estimates of the proportion of field plots meeting the MQO for a region and year are calculated from blind/cold checks by lichen QA specialists (again, different from other FIA indicators) on plots previously sampled by field crew who did not know which plots would be checked. It can be assumed that field samples achieving the field MQO will have within-plot resampling repeatability for richness index of about 35 percent (reasonable given a 65-percent threshold) (Patterson et al., in press). The quality goal for lichen field data is that 90 percent of field samples meet the 65-percent threshold.

Each lichen gradient model establishes within-plot resampling repeatability for lichen response indexes based on data from field samples that meet the measurement quality goal (above). The goals for lichen response indexes from any new model are that indexes from repeat plot samples in the same year differ by 10 to12 percent or less of original gradient length as stated in documentation for that lichen gradient model. Gradient length is defined as largest minus smallest score for plots on that gradient in the published lichen gradient model. These goals have been established from estimates for the first lichen gradient model developed for the

Southeast Lichen Model Region (McCune et al. 1997a, 1997b). Estimated repeatability was found to be 6 to 8 percent for lichen response indexes from three western model regions (Washington and Oregon west of the Cascades crest, Geiser and Neitlich 2007; two California regions, Jovan and McCune 2005, 2006).

If repeatability error for lichen response indexes in a single year is up to 12 percent of gradient length, then a change over time (calculated for repeat samples of a single plot by subtracting one response index from the other) of at least 15 percent is probably needed to suggest that the change exceeds expected sampling error.

In two studies in the Southeast Lichen Model Region, multiple samples from field crew on the same plot who achieved at least 65 percent of an expert's species count had acceptable repeatability (bias 9 to 12 percent of total lichen gradient length and accuracy of 88 to 90 percent as compared with the lichen specialist) for lichen response indexes (McCune et al. 1997a). Based on these calculations and assuming most lichen field samples met the field MQO (not tested for these data sets), within-plot resampling repeatability for lichen response indexes was estimated as approximately 10 to 12 percent for this region as a whole (McCune et al. 1997b). It is estimated based on this repeatability that for this region, a change in lichen response index of at least 15 percent must be seen to suggest it exceeds sample error. Proportion of plots whose change in lichen response indexes exceeds this threshold is reported for lichen climate and air quality indexes in table 4.

Population-Level Attributes

This section has three subsections, listed in order of how tasks should be approached. Presentation of recommended population-level analyses is such an important topic that it is covered in its own separate section that follows. "Appropriate geographic units for analysis" evaluates several criteria for selection of the population to be analyzed. "Screening plots" presents detailed step-wise procedures for screening plots before inclusion in summaries or analyses. "Description of populations" outlines standard descriptive summaries that are useful for presentation in reports even without any further analyses.

Appropriate geographic units for analysis—

A minimum sample size of 10 to 15 plots and a preferred sample size of 30 or more plots are suggested as criteria for selecting grouping units for analysis, although no formal studies have been conducted. The sample size restriction in conjunction with the low spatial density of FIA lichen plots makes some states and other small geographic areas too small to be summary and analysis groups. Both political and ecological geographic units have been used for grouping, depending on purpose. If sufficient data are available, analysts can investigate the feasibility of grouping by additional criteria such as forest characteristics.

Geographic units appropriate for analysis depend upon the attributes being examined. For lichen species richness index, states and FIA regions (primarily for political purposes) or ecoregion provinces, lichen model regions, and larger geographic regions (primarily for ecological purposes) up to and including the entire country, are appropriate units for population estimates. For lichen response indexes, lichen model region and states within lichen model region (primarily for political purposes) or lichen model region and ecoregion provinces within lichen model region (primarily for ecological purposes) are appropriate units for population estimates. Until lichen gradient models are calibrated between model regions, comparison of lichen response indexes between regions is not appropriate.

> The FIA Southeast Lichen Model Region (SE) includes five Southeastern States: Alabama, Georgia, North Carolina, South Carolina, and Virginia. Examples for population-level attributes come from this geographic region that has both political and ecological relevance. NOTE: in figure 3, Virginia is color-coded as being part of the Mid Atlantic Lichen Model Region rather than the SE region. Virginia was included in the SE region, but it is also being included in the Mid Atlantic region (model in development). Virginia's inclusion in both lichen gradient models will facilitate calibration between these two models and adjustment of an appropriate boundary between the two lichen model regions.

Lichen indexes are appropriate for analysis of patterns at large geographic scales.

Screening plots—

Before being included in populations for descriptive summary or analysis, plots should be screened to identify those that do not meet established criteria and might bias results. Screening should proceed by answering questions in this order:

A. Is adequate lichen substrate available?

B. Can the plot be fitted to a lichen gradient model?

C. Is fit to a gradient model adequate?

D. Are plots represented appropriately for the analysis?

If the answer is no to a question, the plot should probably be excluded at that point and screening for that plot should proceed no further. Paragraphs dealing with each type of screening are marked by letter below.

A. If appropriate lichen substrate is extremely sparse on a plot (indicated by very low total basal area of live trees [BA] on an FIA plot), then lichen species richness index may be depressed and plot lichen response indexes may be biased. Lichen gradient model reports include recommendations about whether minimum BA thresholds are linked to effects on lichen indexes. If no lichen gradient model is available, use the following general recommendations. Plots in Eastern States with live tree BA below 5 m^2/ha (21.8 ft^2/acre) appear to have depressed lichen species richness index (McCune et al. 1997b, Will-Wolf et al. 2006, Will-Wolf unpublished data) and biased lichen response indexes (McCune et. al 1997b), so such plots should be considered for exclusion from most analyses. For Western States, no such limitations have been observed (Geiser and Neitlich 2007; Jovan and McCune 2005, 2006), so no default minimum BA threshold is recommended. There is no valid way to adjust plot indexes for limited substrate availability.

B. All lichen plots in a geographic unit or other group may be included for descriptive summary and analysis of lichen species richness index, but not all plots can be assigned lichen response indexes even when a model is completed (see subsection "Assigning response indexes" p. 15). So sample size for a lichen response index may be smaller than for species richness index in the same unit or group.

C. A plot with a lichen response index flagged for poor fit to its model should be considered for exclusion from summary tables or analyses (see subsection "Assigning response indexes" p. 15).

> **Lichen data must be screened before analysis.**

It is recommended that for standard analyses, plots that fail to meet criteria as outlined above be excluded. Plots with indexes affected by temporary within-plot factors such as low BA or those whose lichen response indexes do not accurately reflect plot condition (flags for poor fit) can bias assessment of patterns or trends using the standard approaches recommended below. Inclusion of a very few plots with low tree BA or with flags for poor fit to a lichen gradient model may not materially affect analyses (McCune et al. 1997b). The proportion of plots with low BA (for Eastern States) or flags for poor fit should always be checked before proceeding with any analysis of lichen data, and should be reported regardless of whether those plots are excluded from analyses.

D. The analyst should screen for any resampled plots. The population to be described or analyzed for standard reports should include either plots represented only once, or only plots resampled in all the years to be included for that analysis. For populations that should include plots represented only once (for instance, point-in-time analysis of patterns), data for all but one time for any resampled plots should be excluded according to reasonable and explicitly stated rules. For populations that should include plots resampled in all the years selected, if any plot fails to meet a criterion in any year, that plot must be excluded for all years.

Description of populations—

Both numerical summaries and maps are appropriate tools to describe indexes for populations of plots. Tables present much information in a compact format, and maps are an extremely useful tool to display regional patterns in an attractive and accessible format. Because the density of forest health plots is so low, kriging or other smoothing or interpolation procedures for maps may give inappropriate impressions of data coverage, and may inappropriately suggest smooth gradations of plot indexes where none occur. No nationally consistent general map interpolation procedures are currently appropriate to be recommended for standard reporting of lichen indexes. Dot maps are the currently recommended option; the analyst can display ecoregion provinces or other relevant land classification information in additional layers.

A typical population to use for analysis of lichen indexes is the population of plots found in an appropriate geographic unit or set of units to be compared. Estimates of the form "[lichen index value x] per area" (i.e., per-acre estimates) are not appropriate, because lichen response indexes are unitless numbers and lichen species richness index should be treated as a unitless number. The most appropriate area-based estimates using lichen indexes should be of the type "…for y plots within [geographic unit] of z area, average lichen index is x, or index range is x-x, or average change in index is x." Or within a geographic unit having an area of z, report proportion or percentage of plots in a particular lichen index category, and compare proportions/percentages in the same lichen index categories between geographic units.

For the Southeast Lichen Model Region (SE):

A. Four percent of the 1998 SE region plots and 1.5 percent of the 1999 SE region plots had basal area below the SE model threshold (McCune et al. 1997b) and were excluded from the population summarized in table 2.

B. Two percent of the 1998 plots and 1.2 percent of the 1999 plots in table 2 could not be assigned lichen response indexes, so they were excluded from the population for table 3.

C. Five and three-tenths percent of the 1998 plots and 0.6 percent of the 1999 plots assigned lichen response indexes had flags for poor fit; they were also excluded from table 3.

D. After excluding low BA plots, 1998 and 1999 SE data included 26 plots sampled in both years. The data summarized in tables 2 and 3 include each plot represented only once. If the plot had valid lichen response indexes for only one year, that year represented the plot in both tables. If the plot had valid lichen response indexes for both years, the year with the higher lichen species richness index represented that plot in both tables. For ties on both criteria, the later year represented that plot in both tables. If the plot had flagged lichen response indexes (or none) for both years, the year with the higher lichen species richness index, or the later year if indexes were tied, represented that plot in table 2 only. The above procedure ensured that all plots included for table 3 were also included for table 2 (the latter included 19 more plots than did table 3).

The 1994 and 1998 SE data included 76 plots sampled in both 1994 and 1998 in Alabama, Georgia, and Virginia, all above the low BA cutoff and with lichen response indexes. Of these, 5 plots in 1994 and 4 plots in 1998 had flags for poor fit of response indexes; the 69 plots with valid lichen response indexes for both years were the population analyzed for table 4 and mapped in figure 6.

Descriptive summaries of populations of lichen indexes are quite useful.

The simplest population-level attributes for any geographic unit, or other plot grouping factor such as inventory year, are descriptive summary statistics (mean, median, mode, range) for lichen indexes of all the plots included in that geographic unit, year, or other group. Another useful population-level description of lichen indicator attributes is frequency distribution among categories for a plot-level lichen index within an appropriate grouping unit. Categories for frequency distributions need to be standard for all groups being compared. Appropriate categories for frequency distributions for lichen species richness index and lichen response indexes are established as part of the development of a lichen gradient model. Categories for frequency distribution of lichen species richness index to be compared between lichen model regions or larger geographic units have so far been based on categories developed for the Southeast Lichen Gradient Model (McCune et al. 1997b). This conveniently fosters comparison of frequency distributions for lichen species richness index from different regions of the United States. One additional descriptive statistic useful for the lichen indicator is the change of plot species composition across a region, also called beta diversity or species turnover rate. Calculation of regional composition change by dividing total number of lichen species found in a region by average plot lichen species richness index (McCune and Grace 2002) may be the only method applicable to the FIA lichen indicator.

Tables 2 and 3 present example descriptive summaries for 1998 and 1999 data sets from Alabama, Virginia, and the entire Southeast Lichen Model Region (SE) in which they are embedded. Groups summarized within region could also be based on ecoregions, as shown in figure 5, instead of states. Note that both Eastern Broadleaf province subregions within the SE region (fig. 5) include too few plots to be retained as separate ecoregion groups for analysis should that be desired.

Comparison of populations of plots from multiple years can use two classes of plots: comparison of groups of unique plots sampled in different years, or comparison of the same plots sampled in multiple years. Data for groups of unique plots

Lichen indexes from unique plots sampled in the Southeast region in 1998 and 1999 are summarized in tables 2 and 3. Interpretation of the lichen air quality index is briefly noted after frequency categories in table 3. Lichen species richness index for individual 1998–99 plots is plotted on a map of the region for visual presentation (fig. 5).

sampled in different years are available early in a sampling cycle. If enough plots are available, they can be grouped by both geographic groups and years.

Because plots are currently scheduled to be resampled for lichens at 10-year intervals, data from repeat samples of the same plots are expected to accumulate slowly. However, they support much more precise and therefore more powerful indicators for trend analysis than do comparisons between groups of different plots. Plot-level lichen indexes from repeat samples of the same plots in different years could be summarized as in tables 2 and 3, but statistical analysis is performed with different, more powerful tests on lichen indexes from paired or repeated plots.

For a set of plots sampled at two different times, the difference in plot lichen index from simple subtraction can be summarized similarly to lichen indexes for comparisons across space–presented as tabular data or mapped. The analyst should be explicit and consistent in designating the baseline (older) year and distinguishing it from the year whose indexes are to be subtracted. Averaging change estimates ignoring sign estimates the magnitude of deviations between sample periods, whereas averaging with sign included estimates the magnitude of any trend. High average deviation (ignoring sign) indicates more change. If average trend is very small compared to average deviation, the changes may not represent a coherent regional trend. Based on assessment of repeatability error for lichen response indexes (see subsection "Quality assessment of plot-level indexes" p. 26), finding a low proportion of plots that changed <15 percent of gradient length would suggest there had been notable changes. Reporting proportion of plots in this group for species richness index is much less useful, as the expected variation in species richness index is so high (typically about 35 percent).

Lichen species richness, climate, and air quality indexes for sixty-nine 1998
Southeast Lichen Model Region (SE) plots were subtracted from indexes for
the same plots in 1994 to generate change estimates. Average trend for all
three indexes was positive from 1994 to 1998, indicating decline in indexes
over time (table 4; caption includes notes on data screening); interpretation of
trends is given in footnotes. For lichen climate index, average trend was less
than one-tenth of average deviation, suggesting no concerted trend across the
region. For lichen species richness and air quality indexes, average trend was
about half of average deviation, more consistent with a notable regional trend.
The proportion of plots showing little change (<15 percent) is only slightly
lower for air quality index than for climate index, suggesting this is a weak
indicator of a trend. Change in lichen air quality index is mapped in figure 6
to illustrate trends. Interpretation of the mapped change values is noted in the
figure legend.

Recommended Population-Level Analyses

This discussion focuses on standard analytical approaches that support typical
program reports and maps and are applicable to any FIA lichen data without
further investigation. Reporting of standard products and use of recommended
analyses foster national comparability of results from different regions, and from
different time periods. Some analyses appropriate for data of similar quality at
much higher density are specifically not recommended for standard lichen indicator
data because of the low plot density.

This section has three subsections corresponding to distinct stages of data
analysis. As with earlier sections, steps in analysis are illustrated with representative
data sets from the Southeast Lichen Model Region. "Statistical properties of
indexes" covers evaluation of lichen indexes to see how their characteristics match
with parametric assumptions. "Analysis of indexes" covers recommended default
statistical approaches for standard analyses to limit the workload and the number of
decisions that need to be made by the analyst. "Interpretation of results" suggests
approaches that take into account the limitations of lichen indicator data, as well as
the nature of the chosen analysis methods.

Statistical properties of indexes—

Before applying statistical tests, an analyst should first explore a data set consisting of lichen index values to ensure statistical assumptions for the selected procedures are met. If they are not, the analyst needs to decide what to do—transform data, ignore violations of assumptions, or choose a different kind of analysis (Sokal and Rohlf 1995). Several characteristics of FIA lichen data suggest there are likely to be violations of assumptions for parametric statistical tests. Plot data from any region with a sample size large enough to analyze at all are expected to represent lichen communities that vary systematically with respect to several environmental factors of interest rather than being replicate samples of a homogeneous lichen community. Lichen species richness indexes are count data rather than continuous variables; counts often follow Poisson rather than normal distributions and square-root transformation is often recommended (Sokal and Rohlf 1995).

Three general tests for assumptions of parametric statistical tests (Sokal and Rohlf 1995) were used that could be routinely applied to typical FIA lichen indexes: homogeneity of variances (Levene's test, performed in SPSS 2007), normality (Kolmogorov-Smirnov and Shapiro-Wilk tests, performed in SPSS 2007), and serial independence (performed in Excel 2003). Tests for normality and homogeneity of variances can be performed for index values grouped by years and states. Tests for serial independence can be performed for single or combined years. For a test of serial independence, one orders plots in some reasonable way, such as by sample date or by geographic proximity. The interpretation of lack of serial independence would thus differ with the ordering. For data ordered by date, one would be testing for seasonal variation. Because lichen abundance does not vary by season, a significant result would indicate seasonal variation in crew performance at finding lichens. For data ordered by geographic proximity, significant departure from serial independence is an indication of spatial autocorrelation. This could be expected for most lichen indexes because plot indexes represent lichen community composition that varies along directional environmental gradients.

Populations of lichen indexes often do not meet assumptions for parametric statistical tests.

Southeast Lichen Model Region (SE) lichen plot species richness, climate, and air quality indexes from 1994, 1998, and 1999 (tables 2 and 3) and the subset of plots sampled in both 1994 and 1998 (table 4) were tested for statistical assumptions. For tests of serial independence, plots were ordered by latitude degrees, then longitude degrees, then latitude minutes, then longitude minutes.

Few variables for the full-year data sets met all assumptions and none met all assumptions for both years and states. More than half had non-normal distributions within year or state. Lichen species richness index between states and lichen climate index between years had homogeneous variances–the rest did not. Lichen climate and air quality indexes were never serially independent, whereas lichen species richness index was always serially independent. Lichen indexes for the subset of paired 1994 and 1998 plots met assumptions more often than did the full data sets for those years. Fewer than half were non-normal, all had homogeneous variances between both years and states, and only lichen climate index was not serially independent for one year. The lichen species richness index appeared to meet assumptions more often than did lichen response indexes.

Parametric statistical analyses on original data would probably be appropriate for 1994 and 1998 paired plots, but not for groups of 1998-99 plots. For greater comparability, example analyses are all conducted with analysis of variance on ranked data and with nonparametric tests.

The example data (see text box above) are typical of FIA lichen indexes, so the common and not particularly predictable violations of assumptions seen for the examples are probably also typical of many FIA lichen data sets. Assumption of normality is relevant for analysis of variance (ANOVA) on plots grouped by state and/or year, but not for ANOVA on repeated plot samples with only one replicate per year. Assumptions of homogeneous variances and serial independence are relevant for many kinds of parametric tests including ANOVA, regression, and correlation.

Alternatives to parametric statistical tests are recommended as the standard default procedures for routine analyses; there is then no need to explore whether lichen indexes meet assumptions. A variety of data transformations to reduce violations of assumptions might be considered in different situations depending on the nature of the data. The only data transformation presented here is rank transformation, because it can be recommended for any of the lichen indexes without further evaluation of data. Rank transformation has the further advantage that it automatically standardizes data with different measurement units or ranges of values, so several variables can be included in the same analysis without bias.

For standard FIA reporting, analyzing all lichen data with similar procedures contributes to ease of understanding and comparison of results on an equal basis. Performing individual analyses with the most powerful appropriate statistical procedures, even if these differ for different analyses, introduces an additional element of variation for comparisons and may make results harder to explain. It is also much more time consuming.

Analysis of indexes—

One statistical approach is recommended as the default choice: parametric tests performed on rank-transformed data (Conover and Iman 1981, Yandell 1997). This approach is taken so analysts do not need to test whether assumptions are met before performing standard analyses. Some statistical power is given up with this approach if data actually do meet parametric assumptions, but much time is saved. Appropriate standard nonparametric tests are also mentioned. Nonparametric tests, also known as distribution-free methods, are not sensitive to distribution of either original data or error variance (Sokal and Rohlf 1995). Recommendations for statistical tests were developed after consultation with statistician Brian Yandell of the University of Wisconsin-Madison. Tests for spatial autocorrelation are not recommended for standard FIA analyses because they generally add little new or useful information, given the low density of standard FIA lichen plots and the expectation that plot indexes will often vary systematically along geographical gradients as macroenvironment varies.

Whenever results of more than one statistical test are presented, significance should be evaluated while at least informally taking into account assessment of experiment-wide error. One simple way to do this is to be more conservative when deciding whether results are significant. For instance, one could require a p-value of <0.01 before interpreting the test as showing significant results. Formal procedures to account for experiment-wide error (such as Bonferroni adjustment) can be difficult to apply. One must know to what extent different explanatory factors are independent of one another before applying the formal procedure.

Assessment of strength of patterns across space or between years with non-repeated plots can be conducted with ANOVA on ranked data with unequal sample sizes, or with standard nonparametric tests for randomized groups such as states, ecoregions, or years. One-way ANOVA with unequal sample sizes (with two categories, equivalent to randomized t-test) on ranked data assesses the significance of differences between plots grouped by a single factor. If sample size is large enough, two-way ANOVA with unequal sample sizes on ranked data assesses the significance of differences between plots grouped by two factors, and of an interaction effect. Kruskal-Wallis, Mann Whitney U, or Kolmogorov-Smirnov Z tests assess the significance of differences between plots grouped by a single factor (Lehmann 1975, Sokal and Rohlf 1995), analogous to one-way ANOVA.

Alabama and Virginia for 1998 and 1999 are compared with one-way ANOVA on ranked data for state or year, with two-way ANOVA on ranked data for both state and year (sample sizes borderline for Alabama), and with nonparametric tests for state or year. No significant differences were found between the two states, between years, or between years and states, and year-by-state interaction was not significant. These results are reported in footnotes to tables 2 and 3.

Repeat plot samples can be analyzed with two-way ANOVA without replication on ranked data for plots and years, or with appropriate nonparametric statistical tests. Nonparametric tests appropriate for paired or repeated-measures data to assess the strength of trends between years (Lehmann 1975; Sokal and Rohlf 1995: 440-450) include the Wilcoxon's Signed Rank test or Friedman's test for randomized blocks with years designated as treatments and plots as blocks (a much less powerful test). The Kruskal-Wallis test on plots is also appropriate to test for differences between plots for combined years. When more than two sample times are compared, analysis can include two-way ANOVA without replication on ranked data for the full data set, followed by Wilcoxon's Signed Rank test for particular pairs of years. Until at least four repeat time periods are available, this simpler analysis approach is more appropriate than more complicated time series analyses.

For the Southeast Lichen Model Region example in table 4 with resampled plots, the same population of plots was used for ease of comparison to evaluate trends in lichen species richness, climate, and air quality indexes. More pairs of plots could have been included to evaluate trends in lichen species richness index, and for a standard report an analyst might want to include such additional data. The two-way ANOVA of plots and years is clearly more powerful than conducting equivalent analyses with two different nonparametric tests, and is also more efficient. Plots were not grouped by states as well as year because there are fewer than 30 plots for several cells. Lichen air quality and climate indexes are independent of one another, and lichen species richness index is partially correlated with both, so to account for experiment-wide error (multiple tests on the same data set), probability of <0.02 is interpreted as significant, and of <0.003 is interpreted as highly significant, rather than the single-test standards of <0.05 and <0.01 often used (each of the latter was divided by ~2.5). Many significant differences were found. Since the resampled plot data for table 4 did meet most assumptions for parametric tests, ANOVA on original data was also performed for comparison. The results (not shown) were almost identical, suggesting little power was lost by using ranked data even though most parametric assumptions were met.

Although multiple options for statistical testing are presented and discussed, it is likely that only one of these options would be used by an analyst for standard reporting. Probably the most powerful of the options is ANOVA on ranked data. One-way or two-way ANOVA with unequal sample sizes is recommended for assessment of pattern across space or randomized groups over time with a population of unique plots. Two-way ANOVA without replication is recommended for repeat samples of the same plots. Using ANOVA on ranked data does require one assumption about data distribution not assumed by true nonparametric tests: for ANOVA it is assumed that the magnitude of differences between small-numbered ranks is the same as for equivalent differences between high-numbered ranks (Yandell 1997). Failure to meet this assumption does not invalidate the test, but this assumption does need to be considered when using the original index values for reporting results of a comparison.

To avoid confusion in interpreting the ecological meaning of ranked data, it is recommended that the lowest index value always be given rank 1, so the order of

Analysis of variance for populations of ranked lichen indexes is the recommended analysis tool.

ranks matches the numerical order of the original variable. This standard rule helps the analyst correctly interpret statistical results in terms of the original gradient–warmer vs. cooler climate, better vs. poorer air quality, etc. The greatest potential for confusion occurs with numerical results that have signs on them–correlation coefficients and change estimates, for example.

Variability in species richness index of repeat samples from the same plot can be 35 percent or more and still achieve the minimum standard of at least 65 percent of a lichen expert, whereas variability in lichen response indexes from the same field data is much smaller. So it follows that it is more difficult and requires a stronger signal to detect pattern across a region or change over time in lichen species richness index than in a lichen response index.

Interpretation of results—

Interpretation of results should always be made with the limitations of the FIA data and of each lichen index in mind. Several general limitations analysts should consider are discussed with interpretation of example results. Notes accompanying tables 2 through 4 and captions for figures 5 and 6 serve as examples of appropriate interpretation. Additional guidelines and suggestions for analysts are also included in these notes and captions. For a report, an analyst would include only explanations of results actually presented. Examination of absolute index values may also help to appropriately interpret trends. Summaries for geographic units that do not represent appropriate ecological units (states, for instance) should always be interpreted with care. Estimates of total lichen species found (for a region, state, year, or other grouping unit) are influenced (often in a nonlinear manner) by the number of plots included in the population, so this parameter is appropriate for comparing between grouping units only when numbers of plots are very similar (as in table 2). It is expected that differences between two consecutive years for unique samples from spatially interspersed plots would usually not be significant. Differences between widely spaced years for unique samples from spatially interspersed plots can be tested for trends over time, but these are weaker tests than for repeat plot samples over the same period.

For Alabama and Virginia in 1998–99 (example for groups of unique plots), the lack of any significant differences for lichen species richness or lichen air quality index (tables 2 and 3) supports an interpretation that the two states are quite similar and that there was no important difference between years for either state. The two states are indeed significantly different for lichen climate indexes (data not shown); this is expected from the geographic distance between them.

Lichen species richness index in three Southeast States declined significantly from 1994 to 1998 (table 4–example for resampled plots). Because lichen species richness is affected by many variables, an explanation for this significant decline must be sought by looking at other results, such as trends in lichen response indexes. Note in table 4 that whereas lichen climate index showed no change over time, lichen air quality index declined significantly over time (suggesting air quality became poorer). That suggests the decline in lichen species richness index might have occurred because of deterioration in air quality. Figure 6 shows the decline in lichen air quality index was concentrated in Alabama and Georgia, but it also shows that plots indicating declining air quality in those two states are not all clumped around urban areas and are interspersed with plots indicating no change or improving air quality. Recall that interpretation of a high value of any lichen response index can be arbitrary, so the analyst must refer to the documentation for a particular lichen gradient model for aid in interpretation of indexes and trends.

Note also in table 3 that Alabama had a higher proportion of "clean air" plots and a lower proportion of "dirty air" plots than did Virginia in 1998–99, even though Alabama had more plots with declines in air quality (fig. 6). All of these observations suggest that alternate explanations for species richness decline should be investigated. If quality assessment data were available for those years (they are not), one would want to check that most plot data met the field measurement quality objective (MQO) in both years. If, for instance, 90 percent of 1994 blind/cold checks met the field MQO but only 30 percent of 1998 blind/cold checks met the field MQO, then the 1998 lichen air quality indexes could not be assumed to be as reliable as desired, and an analyst might consider discounting the apparent decline as an effect of lower data quality in 1998. A similarly careful evaluation of analysis results is appropriate in all cases before moving to the next step of recommending further investigation of an indicated trend.

Core Tables and Maps

Core tables are defined for the lichen indicator that eventually will be incorporated into the FIA database and may be automatically displayed for selected grouping units (probably states) on the FIA Web site. For one to several geographic groups in a region with lichen data, a core table similar to table 2 can be populated that also incorporates results of appropriate statistical tests. For a region with a lichen gradient model developed, a core table similar to table 3 can be populated for each lichen response index. Gradient models developed to date have identified one lichen air quality response and one to three important lichen climate gradients in a region. The statistical procedures recommended above should be employed as the default options.

Summary core tables and maps are recommended for inclusion in standard reports.

Typically a reporting unit chooses their own boundaries for a geographic group in a core table; it is preferable that they also include the entire lichen model region for comparison (as in fig. 5). Some Eastern States are so small that even after a full sampling cycle is completed there are not enough plots in the state for a reliable statistical unit. Some Midwestern and Western States are large enough that after a full sampling cycle is completed there are enough plots to support summary and analysis by subgroups within the state. For many Western States, one state will include parts of two or more different lichen model regions (e.g., Washington and Oregon in fig. 3). Because lichen response indexes are comparable only within their own lichen model region, summaries of lichen response indexes for different lichen model regions within a state need to be presented separately.

When enough repeat plot samples are available, a core table similar to table 4 can be populated for each lichen index defined for the region, reporting results of ANOVA on ranked data as the default statistical test. Comparisons of nonpaired groups of plots across time, such as comparing lichen indexes for plots in one year with those of plots in another year for the same geographic area, is a much weaker comparison for trend analysis. Large sample sizes are needed for the latter to ensure that significant patterns actually represent trends of interest and are not related to unintended differences between sets of plots in different years. This means that only quite large geographic units are appropriate as grouping factors for such summary statistics. Because of the limitations on geographic application of regional lichen response indexes, nonpaired comparisons are probably most useful for lichen species richness index summarized over entire lichen model regions or even larger units.

Any one set of lichen indexes for plots in a single year or estimates of change over time may also be grouped into a few categories and then single plots mapped by category membership across appropriate geographic units like those in figure 3. Ecoregion province boundaries and state boundaries are two appropriate mapping layers for core maps when individual plot lichen indexes are mapped. Core maps are extremely useful adjuncts to core tables, because visual interpretation is so intuitive.

Tables 2 through 4 and figures 5 and 6 are example core products for standard reporting of lichen indicator data for Southeast States 1994 through 1999. Columns for additional states could be added to tables 2 and 3. Alternately, analyses of patterns could be presented for the region and for three ecoregion groups with adequate sample size (see fig. 5). Separate trend analyses for each of the three states included for table 4 could possibly be presented in separate tables. Separate trend analysis for the Southeastern Mixed Forest ecoregion would be possible; sample size is too small for all other ecoregion groups (see fig. 6).

Standard FIA reporting (detection monitoring results) may highlight problem areas where notable impact to lichen communities appears to have occurred. Such a finding may then trigger the development of a special project (evaluation monitoring) to investigate the problem in greater detail. No evaluation monitoring outputs result automatically from this indicator.

Guidelines for Additional and Future Analyses

It is expected that needs for additional reporting on standard plot data beyond standard products and for supplemental investigations will arise in response to regional needs and to special situations.

Subsection "Analysis for Additional Research and Reporting" reviews a variety of follow-up research approaches that might be triggered from analysis of standard FIA data. "Combined Analyses with Other FIA Indicators" reviews this promising avenue for additional analysis of standard data. There are currently no recommended standard approaches, but research is beginning. "Research Needs for Future Standard Analyses" identifies research needed to support development of improved methods for conducting standard analyses and reporting.

Analysis for Additional Research and Reporting

The possibilities for additional analyses of FIA lichen indicator data are many, and the desire for additional analyses is expected to differ by region depending on particular circumstances and needs (e.g., Jovan 2008). Data users outside the FIA Program also find uses for these data. Many additional and more sophisticated analysis approaches and techniques might be appropriate. However, all data users should keep in mind the basic characteristics and limitations of FIA lichen data as outlined here. Application of the wide toolkit of analysis tools available is limited only by their suitability for FIA lichen data. Whenever an analysis focuses on lichen species composition data and FIA data from multiple years are to be combined, the analyst must first consult the current REF_LICHEN_SPECIES_COMMENTS table. A version of the table that matches the most recent inventory year of data posted on the FIA Web site is also posted there (USDA FS 2010a); more recent versions may be available from the indicator advisor or from an FIA information management office. If taxonomic usage for included species has changed over the data years, the analyst modifies data according to instructions in the table so the multiple years can be appropriately analyzed together.

For FIA-quality lichen data where plots occur at much higher density, more sophisticated mapping tools–modeling, kriging, and other interpolation methods for producing continuous mapped surfaces–may well be appropriate. Geiser and Neitlich (2007) presented excellent examples of kriged map products supported by standard FIA lichen data from plots much more dense than the standard FIA plot network. Where plot density is much higher, investigation of spatial autocorrelation may have pertinent applications as well.

Detection from standard analyses of an unexpected spatial pattern, an indication of a localized problem, or a significant trend over time may be followed by a more detailed analysis to investigate the phenomenon. Standard maps are particularly useful to aid in visual identification of a geographically localized problem. Special projects involving additional field sampling may be one way to address the investigation. For instance, the unexpected occurrence of a cluster of low air quality indexes in northwest Colorado indicated by standard analysis (detection monitoring in FIA) of permanent plot data (McCune et al. 1998) triggered a more intensive FHM evaluation monitoring project. Study of the local region included collection of data on additional plots using the FIA protocol (Peterson and Neitlich 2001). Additional sampling tools, such as collection of lichen tissue samples for analysis of heavy metals and other elements, may also be appropriate for such special projects.

FIA lichen data and indexes are useful for much more than the recommended standard analyses.

More sophisticated analyses might be appropriate for regions having more data, or in the future when more cycles of repeat sampling have been completed. An analyst could apply more sophisticated tools or more detailed analyses (e.g., multi-variate community analyses, statistical analyses of individual species or groups) using the original data sets of species abundance at standard plots for more intensive investigations of relations with standard lichen indexes. One could explore lichen species relations with environmental factors other than those represented by lichen response indexes from standard models (e.g., Will-Wolf et al. 2006). Or one could analyze plot lichen indexes grouped in nonstandard ways such as by nearby land use. Multiyear data sets could be used to investigate relations of lichen species composition to local plot factors such as tree species composition or disturbance history, if more intensive data sets are not available for the area. Results of studies that focus on local factors should always be interpreted with the limitations of FIA lichen data in mind: field protocol is designed to reduce signal from local and within-plot variation, abundance data are imprecise, the timed sample represents a probably biased subset of the lichen community at a site, etc.

Comparison of intensive local studies with the extensive FIA data sets provides consistent context for the local study. Use of the FIA lichen indicator sampling protocol as well as any other lichen sampling protocol on at least a subset of the area in an intensive local study supports robust quantitative linkage of results from the local study to FIA data and to other local studies. This linkage can promote better extrapolation of the results of the more local or more intensive study to a broader context, leading to wider application of the results.

A commonly desired use for FIA lichen data by outside data users is contribution to mapping of individual species distributions. Consulting the FIA lichen reference tables is particularly important for such projects, to clearly understand definitions of and changes in taxonomic usage in the FIA Program. These data users should also consider the limitations of the FIA field sampling and should consult the specialist manuals (see subsection "Sample identification and data recording," p. 13) to understand lichen species naming and species identification protocols used in the program. A lichen species name used in the FIA Program may also refer to specimens of look-alike species not distinguishable with the standard FIA identification protocol. For range mapping, presence of a lichen species is an unequivocal data record, but absence from a timed survey by a nonspecialist is a much more tentative data record.

Combined Analyses With Other FIA Indicators

Research on combining FIA indicators to develop stronger indexes of response to environmental drivers such as pollution and climate will facilitate addressing broad forest health assessment issues, an important goal of the FIA Program. Any protocols developed must be tested in multiple geographic regions to see if nationally consistent protocols for combining indicators are supported. Any of the FIA lichen indexes may be compared with any other FIA plot-level variable, for instance via correlation or regression to assess whether they vary together and have potential to address causal relationships. Such analyses are not currently considered standard products, but they are indeed appropriate for application in all FIA regions. The strongest analyses will result from comparison of trends in lichen indexes with those of other forest health and forest mensuration indicators from the same population of plots. These efforts will be more robust when the number of plots resampled for lichens has increased. The lichen species richness index may be compared with other plot-level indicators at any scale from small regions on up to the entire country as long as sample size is adequate. However, lichen response indexes may be used only within their own lichen model region.

Restrictions similar to those discussed above in subsection "Statistical properties of indexes" (p. 35) apply to use of lichen indexes in combination with other FIA variables. Rank transformation of data would be particularly helpful here, to standardize across different units of measurement, as well as to cope with any failure to meet statistical assumptions.

Some kinds of analyses are particularly recommended. Any FIA plot-level variable that is considered to reflect forest health is appropriate to compare with a lichen air quality index or a combined air quality index that includes lichens. Plot-level integrations of crown condition, damage, disease, and mortality variables are likely candidates. Comparison with general plot-level summaries of degree of damage or disease may generate more useful results than comparisons with specific causal agents. This approach can address questions of whether air quality is a potential contributing factor to susceptibility of forest trees to disease or damage in general. A pilot analysis using this approach (Will-Wolf and Jovan 2008) suggested a potential link between the lichen air quality index and forest health for an Eastern Broadleaf ecoregion. Comparison with variables representing understory vegetation can address questions of whether air quality is a potential contributing factor to low understory plant species diversity or to invasion by exotics. Until calibration of lichen air quality indexes between lichen model regions has been completed, such combined air quality investigations need to be conducted within individual lichen model regions.

Another useful analysis would be to explore response to climate drivers by a number of forest ecosystem components including lichens, soils, understory vegetation, and forest mensuration indicators. Such an analysis could compare the strength and spatial scale of variation in response to climate of the different indicators and highlight those potentially most sensitive to climate change. This in turn could lead to indexes of climate response that combine fast versus slow climate responders and development from FIA data of general indicators of susceptibility to climate change. Comparison with forest health variables such as those listed above may also help address questions of how climate interacts with other factors to potentially contribute to susceptibility of forests to disease, damage, invasion by exotics, or alteration in biodiversity.

Research Needs for Future Standard Analyses—
Four distinct areas have been identified where further research is needed to develop better analysis tools for standard evaluation of FIA lichen data. Other areas will no doubt arise in the future. Subsections "Sensitivity analysis for lichen indexes," "Mapping techniques," "Calibration between gradient models," and "Bayesian analysis" outline identified research needs. Whenever improvement of standard analyses is the goal, the choice of analysis tools to be investigated should be constrained by the need for FIA analysts to use widely available and thoroughly tested software and by the applicability of the tools to FIA lichen data and analysis needs nationwide.

Sensitivity analysis for lichen indexes—
Formal sensitivity analysis of lichen indexes would be useful to improve understanding of detection limits for pattern and trend analysis. A lower limit for the amount of variation needed to detect a pattern, or change needed to detect a trend, is set by repeatability of multiple samples of the same plot (variation from random or nontarget sources). It is of course expected that sample size will affect detection ability, and it would be useful to quantify that relationship. Such analyses would support more robust recommendations about needed sample sizes.

Mapping techniques—
Guidelines for interpolation procedures to produce smoothed distributions on maps need to be developed for the FIA Program. They should include guidelines for data

density as well as evaluations of the effectiveness and reliability of different approaches to generating interpolated maps. Guidelines for data density might differ for maps of different spatial extent. For instance, it might be decided that it is appropriate to interpolate for maps covering an entire FIA region or the entire United States, but not for maps covering smaller areas. The appearance of smoothing might be considered more misleading at smaller spatial scales. There is no current expectation that guidelines and procedures appropriate for generating interpolated maps will be developed for the standard forest health plot grid, but the investigation should occur.

Calibration between gradient models—

After FIA lichen gradient models have been developed for adjacent regions, a logical next step is to calibrate lichen response indexes from these adjacent models so evaluation of response to the underlying environmental drivers can be conducted at larger geographic scales. One reasonable approach is to fit plots near the shared model region boundaries to both adjacent models and calibrate the lichen response indexes from the two models for the same plot. An outcome of such research may well be to reevaluate the permanent assignment of a plot to a particular lichen model region. Reassigning border plots may result in more ecologically relevant and more stable boundaries for lichen model regions. This may also result in greater precision in detection of patterns and trends in response to environmental drivers.

Bayesian analysis—

Bayesian approaches to statistical analysis are becoming increasingly popular in an academic research context. Their appropriateness for analysis of standard FIA lichen indexes should be explored, and their reliability compared to standard statistical tests should be evaluated. Such approaches may well be found to be superior to currently recommended techniques for some applications. However, demonstrably superior techniques should be recommended for standard analyses only after reliable software and simple, easy-to-follow protocols for their use are widely available to FIA analysts.

Acknowledgments

Funding was provided under cooperative agreements between Southern Research Station Forest Inventory and Analysis (SRS-FIA) and the University of Wisconsin-Madison (UW-Madison). The author was FIA lichen indicator co-advisor 1995–2001, advisor 2002–2007, co-advisor 2008–2009, and is developing two FIA lichen region gradient models.

The recommended analysis procedures and early versions of this report have been much improved through discussions and extensive edits from William Bechtold (SRS-FIA), an FIA Lichen Indicator "Statistical Band buddy," as well as from several other FIA statisticians and analysts. Statistical consultant Brian Yandell (UW-Madison) suggested the use of ranked data and gave extensive advice on appropriate analyses. All FIA lichen gradient model developers past and present have contributed to improvements in FIA lichen data analysis. Bruce McCune (Oregon State University) and Peter Neitlich (National Park Service) contributed many helpful comments on earlier versions of the report. Sarah Jovan (Pacific Northwest FIA and OSU) commented on several versions of the report and shared in making decisions that improved the final product. Three anonymous reviewers contributed critical and insightful reviews of the report. Paul Patterson (Interior West FIA), FIA Statistical Band editor for this report, has made many helpful comments on every version of the report and has contributed much guidance throughout the process. Peter Neitlich and Kandis Elliot (UW-Madison) created figures, and John Wolf (UW-Madison, retired) edited the text. The final product is the responsibility of the author.

English Equivalents

1 hectare (ha) = 2.47 acres (ac)

1 kilometer (km) = 0.621 mile (mi)

1 meter (m) = 3.28 feet (ft)

1 m^2/ha = 4.37 ft^2/ac

References

Arseneault, D.; Payette, S. 1992. A postfire shift from lichen-spruce to lichen-tundra vegetation at tree line. Ecology. 73: 1067–1081.

Bailey, R.G.; Avers, P.E.; King, T.; NcNab, W.H. 1994. Ecoregions and subregions of the United States (map). Washington, DC: U.S. Geological Survey. Scale 1:7,500,000. Colored. Accompanied by a supplementary table of map unit scale descriptions compiled and edited by McNab, W.H. and Bailey, R.G. Prepared for the USDA Forest Service.

Bates, J.W.; Farmer, A.M., eds. 1992. Bryophytes and lichens in a changing environment. Oxford, United Kingdom: Clarendon Press. 404 p.

Belnap, J.; Lange, O.L. 2005. Biological soil crusts and global changes: What does the future hold? In: Dighton, J.; White, J.F.; Oudemans, P., eds. The fungal community: its organization and role in the ecosystem. 3rd ed. Boca Raton, FL: CRC Press, Taylor & Francis: 697–712.

Cleland, D.T.; Freeouf, J.A.; Keys, J.E.; Nowacki, G.J.; Carpenter, C.A.; McNab, W.H. 2005. Ecological subregions: sections and subsections for the conterminous United States. A.M. Sloan, tech. ed. Washington, DC: U.S. Department of Agriculture, Forest Service. Map, presentation scale 1:3,500,000; colored. Also on CD-ROM as a GIS coverage in ArcINFO format.

Conover, W.J.; Iman, R.L. 1981. Rank transformations as a bridge between parametric and nonparametric statistics. The American Statistician. 35: 124–129.

Dawson, W.R.; Ligon, J.D.; Murphy, J.R.; Myers, J.P.; Simberloff, D.; Verner, J. 1987. Report of the scientific advisory panel on the spotted owl. Condor. 89: 205–229.

de Wit, T. 1983. Lichens as indicators of air quality. Environmental Monitoring and Assessment. 3: 273–282.

Dietrich, M.; Scheidegger, C. 1997. Frequency, diversity and ecological strategies of epiphytic lichens in the Swiss central plateau and the pre-Alps. Lichenologist. 29: 237–258.

Ellis, C.J.; Coppins, B.J.; Dawson, T.P.; Seaward, M.R.D. 2007. Response of British lichens to climate change scenarios: trends and uncertainties in the projected impact for contrasting biogeographic groups. Biological Conservation. 140: 217–235.

Fenn, M.E.; Baron, J.S.; Allen, E.B.; Rueth, H.M.; Nydick, K.R.; Geiser, L.; Bowman, W.D.; Sickman, J.O.; Meixner, T.; Johnson, D.W.; Neitlich, P. 2003. Ecological effects of nitrogen deposition in the Western United States. BioScience. 53(4): 404–420.

Geiser, L.H.; Neitlich, P. 2007. Air pollution and climate gradients in western Oregon and Washington indicated by epiphytic macrolichens. Environmental Pollution. 145: 203–218.

Green, R.H. 1979. Sampling design and statistical methods for environmental biologists. New York: John Wiley and Sons. 257 p.

Hawksworth, D.L.; Rose, F. 1976. Lichens as pollution monitors. London: Edward Arnold. 60 p.

Jovan, S. 2008. Lichen bioindication of biodiversity, air quality, and climate: baseline results from monitoring in Washington, Oregon, and California. Gen. Tech. Rep. PNW-GTR-737. Portland, OR: U.S. Department of Agriculture, Forest Service, Pacific Northwest Research Station. 115 p. http://www.fs.fed.us/pnw/pubs/pnw_gtr737.pdf. (May 2009).

Jovan, S. 2009. Baseline results from the Lichen Community Indicator in the Pacific Northwest: air quality patterns and evidence of a nitrogen problem. In: Ambrose, M.J.; Conkling, B.L. Forest Health Monitoring 2006 National Technical Report. Gen. Tech. Rep. SRS-117. Asheville, NC: U.S. Department of Agriculture, Forest Service, Southern Research Station. Chap. 5.

Jovan, S.; McCune, B. 2004. Regional variation in epiphytic macrolichen communities in northern and central California forests. Bryologist. 107: 328–339.

Jovan, S.; McCune, B. 2005. Air-quality bioindication in the greater Central Valley of California, with epiphytic macrolichen communities. Ecological Applications. 15: 1712–1726.

Jovan, S.; McCune, B. 2006. Using epiphytic macrolichen communities for biomonitoring ammonia in forests of the Greater Sierra Nevada, California. Water, Air, and Soil Pollution. 170: 69–93.

Legendre, P.; Legendre, L. 1998. Numerical ecology. 2nd English ed. Developments in Environmental Modeling, 20. New York: Elsevier. 853 p.

Lehmann, E.L. 1975. Nonparametrics: statistical methods based on ranks. San Francisco: Holden-Day. 457 p. Also see revised edition by Lehmann, E.L.; D'Abrera, H.J.M. 1988. McGraw Hill.

Lesica, P.; McCune, B.; Cooper, S.; Hong, W.S. 1991. Differences in lichen and bryophyte communities between old-growth and managed second-growth forests. Canadian Journal of Botany. 69: 1745–1755.

Maser, C.; Maser, Z.; Witt, J.W.; Hunt, G. 1986. The northern flying squirrel: a mycophagist in southwestern Oregon. Canadian Journal of Zoology. 64: 2086–2089.

Maser, Z.; Maser, C.; Trappe, J.M. 1985. Food habits of the northern flying squirrel (*Glaucomys sabrinus*) in Oregon. Canadian Journal of Zoology. 63: 1084–1088.

McCune, B. 2000. Lichen communities as indicators of forest health. The Bryologist. 103: 353–356.

McCune, B.; Dey, J.P.; Peck, J.E.; Cassell, D.; Heiman, K.; Will-Wolf, S.; Neitlich, P.N. 1997a. Repeatability of community data: species richness versus gradient scores in large-scale lichen studies. The Bryologist. 100: 40–46.

McCune, B.; Dey, J.P.; Peck, J.E.; Heiman, K.; Will-Wolf, S. 1994. Lichen communities. In: Lewis, T.E.; Conkling, B.L., eds. Forest health monitoring. Southeast loblolly/shortleaf pine demonstration interim report. Washington, DC: Office of research and development, U.S. Environmental Protection Agency: 8.1-8.32. Chap. 8.

McCune, B.; Dey, J.P.; Peck, J.E.; Heiman, K.; Will-Wolf, S. 1997b. Regional gradients in lichen communities of the Southeast United States. The Bryologist. 100: 145–158.

McCune, B.; Grace, J.B. 2002. Analysis of ecological communities. Gleneden Beach, OR: MjM Software Design. 300 p.

McCune, B.; Rogers, P.; Ruchty, A.; Ryan, B. 1998. Lichen communities for forest health monitoring in Colorado, USA. Report to the USDA Forest Service. Ogden, UT: U.S. Department of Agriculture Forest Service, Rocky Mountain Research Station. 98 p.

Muir, P.S.; McCune, B. 1988. Lichens, tree growth, and foliar symptoms of air pollution: Are the stories consistent? Journal of Environmental Quality. 17: 361–370.

Nash, T.H., III, ed. 2008. Lichen biology. 2nd ed. Cambridge, United Kingdom: Cambridge University Press. 486 p.

Nash, T.H., III; Wirth, V., eds. 1988. Lichens, bryophytes and air quality. Bibliotheca Lichenologica 30. Berlin-Stuttgart, Germany: J. Cramer in der Gebruder Borntraeger Verlagsbuchhandlung. 297 p.

National Acidic Deposition Program [NADP]. 2010. Ionic deposition maps. www.nadp.gov. (March 2010).

National Acid Precipitation Assessment Program [NAPAP]. 1991. Acidic deposition: state of science and technology reports. Volumes I-IV. Washington, DC: U.S. Government Printing Office.

Nimis, P.L.; Scheidegger, C.; Wolseley, P., eds. 2002. Monitoring with lichens–monitoring lichens. Introduction. NATO Science Series. The Hague, The Netherlands: Kluwer Academic Publishers. 424 p.

Palmer, M.W.; White, P. S. 1994. Scale dependence and the species-area relationship. The American Naturalist. 144: 717–740.

Patterson, P.; Will-Wolf, S.; Trest, M.T. [In press]. FIA lichen indicator–analysis of QA data. In: Westphal, J., ed. Forest Inventory and Analysis national assessment of data quality for forest health indicators. Gen. Tech. Rep. St. Paul, MN: U.S. Department of Agriculture Forest Service, Northern Research Station: Chap. 3.

Peckarsky, B.L. 1984. Sampling the stream benthos. In: Dowling, J.A.; Rigler, F.H., eds. A manual on methods for the assessment of secondary productivity in fresh waters. 2nd ed. London: Blackwell: 131-160. Chap. 4.

Peet, R.K. 1974. The measurement of species diversity. Annual Review of Ecology and Systematics. 5: 285–307.

Peterson, E.B.; Neitlich, P. 2001. Impacts of two coal-fired power plants on lichen communities in northwestern Colorado. FHM Evaluation Monitoring Study. Internal report to Interior West Region. Ogden, UT: U.S. Department of Agriculture Forest Service, Rocky Mountain Research Station. 34 p.

Pielou, E.C. 1975. Ecological diversity. New York: Wiley. 165 p.

Pike, L.H. 1978. The importance of epiphytic lichens in mineral cycling. Bryologist. 81: 247–257.

Pollard, J.E.; Palmer, C.J. 1998. Forest health monitoring 1998 plot component quality assurance implementation plan. On file with: Research Triangle Park, NC: U.S. Department of Agriculture, Forest Service, National Forest Health Monitoring Program. 17 p.

Richardson, D.H.S. 1988. Understanding the pollution sensitivity of lichens. Botanical Journal of the Linnean Society. 96(1): 31–43.

Rominger, E.M.; Oldemeyer, J.L. 1989. Early-winter habitat of woodland caribou, Selkirk Mountains, British Columbia. Journal of Wildlife Management. 53: 238–243.

Seaward, M.R.D. 1993. Lichens and sulphur dioxide air pollution: field studies. Environmental Review. 1: 73–91.

Servheen, G.; Lyon, L.J. 1989. Habitat use by woodland caribou in the Selkirk Mountains. Journal of Wildlife Management. 53: 230–237.

Sharnoff, S.; Rosentreter, R.R. 2008. Lichen use by wildlife in North America [and] Lichens and invertebrates: a brief review and bibliography. http://www.lichen.com/animals.html. (September 2008).

Showman, R.E. 1992. Lichen studies along a wet sulfate deposition gradient in Pennsylvania. The Bryologist. 95: 166–170.

Sillett, S.C.; Neitlich, P.N. 1996. Emerging themes in epiphyte research in westside forests with special reference to cyanolichens. Northwest Science. 70: 54–60.

Smith, C.; Geiser, L.; Gough, L.; McCune, B.; Ryan, B.; Showman, R. 1993. Species and communities. In: Stolte, K.; Mangis, D.; Doty, R.; Tonnessen, K.; Huckaby, L.S., eds. Lichens as bioindicators of air quality. Gen. Tech. Rep. RM-224. Fort Collins, CO: U.S. Department of Agriculture Forest Service, Rocky Mountain Research Station: 41–66. Chap. 4.

Søchting, U. 2004. *Flavoparmelia caperata*—a probable indicator of increased temperatures in Denmark. Graphis Scripta. 15(1/2): 53–56.

Sokal, R.R.; Rohlf, F.J. 1995. Biometry. 3rd ed. New York: W.H. Freeman & Co. 887 p.

U.S. Department of Agriculture, Forest Service [USDA FS]. 2004. Forest Inventory and Analysis national core field guide. Volume 2: field data collection procedures for phase 3 plots. Version 2.0. Internal report. On file with: USDA Forest Service, Forest Inventory and Analysis, Rosslyn Plaza, 1620 North Kent Street, Arlington, VA 22209.

U.S. Department of Agriculture, Forest Service [USDA FS]. 2010a. Forest Inventory and Analysis. FIA DataMart. http://fiatools.fs.fed.us/fido/index.html. (March 2010).

U.S. Department of Agriculture, Forest Service [USDA FS]. 2010b. Forest Inventory and Analysis national core field guide. FIA field methods for phase 3 measurements. Version 3.0. http://fia.fs.fed.us/library/field-guides-methods-proc/. (March 2010). On file with: USDA Forest Service, Forest Inventory and Analysis, Rosslyn Plaza, 1620 North Kent Street, Arlington, VA 22209.

van Dobben, H.F. 1993. Vegetation as a monitor for deposition of nitrogen and acidity. The Netherlands: Utrecht University. 214 p. Ph.D. dissertation.

van Dobben, H.F.; ter Braak, C.J.F. 1998. Effect of atmospheric NH_3 on epiphytic lichens in the Netherlands: the pitfalls of biological monitoring. Atmospheric Environment. 32: 551–557.

Will-Wolf, S. 1988. Quantitative approaches to air quality studies. In: Nash, T.H., III; Wirth, V., eds. Lichens, bryophytes and air quality. Bibliotheca Lichenologica 30. Berlin-Stuttgart, Germany: J. Cramer in der Gebruder Borntraeger Verlagsbuchhandlung: 109–140.

Will-Wolf, S. 2007. Forest Inventory and Analysis Program lichen specialist training and QA procedures. http://fia.fs.fed.us/lichen/methods/. (March 2010). On file with: Sarah Jovan, FIA lichen indicator advisor, USDA Forest Service, Forestry Sciences Lab, 620 SW Main, Suite 400, Portland, OR 97205.

Will-Wolf, S. 2009. Forest Inventory and Analysis Program lichen specialist identification procedures. http://fia.fs.fed.us/lichen/methods/. (March 2010). On file with: Sarah Jovan, FIA lichen indicator advisor, USDA Forest Service, Forestry Sciences Lab, 620 SW Main, Suite 400, Portland, OR 97205.

Will-Wolf, S.; Geiser, L.H.; Neitlich, P.; Reis, A. 2006. Comparison of lichen community composition with environmental variables at regional and subregional geographic scales. Journal of Vegetation Science. 17: 171–184.

Will-Wolf, S.; Hawksworth, D.L.; McCune, B.; Sipman, H.J.M.; Rosentreter, R. 2004. Assessing the biodiversity of lichenized fungi. In: Mueller, G.M.; Bills, G.F.; Foster, M.S., eds. Biodiversity of fungi: standard methods for inventory and monitoring. San Diego, CA: Elsevier: 173–195.

Will-Wolf, S.; Jovan, S. 2008. Lichens, ozone, and forest health—exploring cross-indicator analyses with FIA data. In: McWilliams, W.; Moisen, G.; Czaplewski, R., comps. 2008. 2008 Forest Inventory and Analysis (FIA) Symposium. Proc. RMRS-P-56. [1 CD]. Fort Collins, CO: U.S. Department of Agriculture, Forest Service, Rocky Mountain Research Station. 18 p. http://www.treesearch.fs.fed.us/pubs/33326. (July 2009).

Will-Wolf, S.; Neitlich, P. 2007. Training manual: the lichen community indicator in FIA and FHM. USDA Forest Service, FIA Program. 100 p. On file with: Sarah Jovan, FIA lichen indicator co-advisor (West), USDA Forest Service, Forestry Sciences Lab, 620 SW Main, Suite 400, Portland, OR 97205.

Will-Wolf, S.; Neitlich, P. 2010. Development of lichen response indexes using a regional gradient modeling approach for large-scale monitoring of forests. Gen. Tech. Rep. PNW-GTR-807. Portland, OR: U.S. Department of Agriculture Forest Service, Pacific Northwest Research Station. 65 p.

Will-Wolf, S.; Neitlich, P.; Esseen, P.-A. 2002a. Monitoring biodiversity and ecosystem function: forests. In: Nimis, P.L.; Scheidegger, C.; Wolseley, P., eds. Monitoring with lichens–monitoring lichens. NATO Science Series. The Hague, The Netherlands: Kluwer Academic Publishers: 203–222.

Will-Wolf, S.; Scheidegger, C.; McCune, B. 2002b. Methods for monitoring biodiversity and ecosystem function. In: Nimis, P.L.; Scheidegger, C.; Wolseley, P., eds. Monitoring with lichens–monitoring lichens. NATO Science Series. The Hague, The Netherlands: Kluwer Academic Publishers: 147–162.

Yandell, B.S. 1997. Practical data analysis for designed experiments. New York, USA: Chapman & Hall. 437 p.

Appendix: Example Standard Lichen Data Upload File

This example lichen laboratory data file excerpted from Will-Wolf (2009) is in the format used for submission to a Forest Inventory and Analysis region information management specialist for uploading to the internal FIA database (NIMS). The private 7-digit P3 HEXID (Forest Health Monitoring HEXID) is the required plot identifier for uploading lichen lab data to NIMS. The 7-digit numbers in the examples below are synthetic numbers in appropriate format: they are **not** valid FIA plot identifiers. Lichen data in the public FIA database (FIADB) on the Web have plots identified by state-county-public plot number. A single plot record consists of the plot identifier on one line plus pairs of numbers on one or more following lines ending with a forward slash. Each pair of numbers is a 3- or 4-digit lichen species code followed by an abundance code. An abundance code of 0.01 signals an "accidental" species record (not deliberately collected by the field technician); it is converted to an abundance of 3 after upload because abundances of 3 are by far the most common value in such data (Will-Wolf 2009). A record with a plot identifier followed on the next line by just a forward slash signals a plot searched and found to have no lichens. Three groups of plots (states) are distinguished in this file.

Example of a standard laboratory data upload file, submitted in ASCII text format:

BREAK
AZ
2218515
2704 3 4017 0.01 4002 3 5701 3 5705 3 8000 3 8214 3 8203 1 /
2218536
2704 3 4017 3 5701 0.01 1008 0.01 5705 3 5723 3 5801 0.01 6303 3 8041 3 8203 3 /
1318652
2704 3 4004 1 4017 3 5701 3 5705 3 8044 3 8203 2 /
BREAK
NV
2318326
2704 3 4017 3 5701 1 5705 3 8041 2 8203 2 5605 0.01 /
2318365
5602 3 5605 3 5705 3 8203 2 /

2318763

/

2318623

2704 3 4017 3 5701 2 5705 3 5611 0.01 8000 3 8214 3 /

2318647

607 3 610 3 8152 2 1200 2 2704 3 4017 3 4004 0.01 4800 3 5201 3 5612 3 5600 3

5611 3

5701 2 5906 3 6303 3 6920 3 8044 3 3106 3 /

2318724

610 0.01 4017 3 5723 3 5701 3 8044 3 8203 3 8214 3 8041 0.01 9000 3 /

BREAK

WY

1318864

4002 3 5705 3 8214 2 8203 3 /

1381888

4017 3 /

1318477

2704 3 4017 3 4806 3 5907 2 5707 3 5705 3 5701 2 8041 3 8203 3 8214 3 /

1318512

4004 3 4017 0.01 5701 3 5705 3 8214 3 8044 3 /

Glossary

application phase—The second phase in implementation of the lichen indicator in the Forest Inventory and Analysis (FIA) Program. In this phase, lichen data are collected from standard FIA plots and are assigned indexes for response to environmental factors defined from an existing regional "FIA lichen gradient model." Many analyses based on these indexes are possible in this phase.

calibration phase—The first phase of implementation of the lichen indicator in the FIA Program. In this phase, lichen data are collected from standard FIA plots and limited analyses are conducted. Supplemental data are collected and an "FIA lichen gradient model" for a particular "FIA lichen model region" is developed. This phase lasts for a region until a gradient model is completed and implemented.

core map—A map showing lichen indicator data that is constructed following a standard template recommended for use in typical state and regional reports for any part of the country.

core table—A table displaying lichen indicator data that is constructed following a standard template recommended for use in typical state and regional reports for any part of the country. It is intended that eventually many steps in production of core tables from data archived in databases will be automated.

FHM—The Forest Health Monitoring Program in the United States Forest Service. Current focus is nationwide reports and special projects.

FIA—The Forest Inventory and Analysis Program in the United States Forest Service. Responsible for nationwide collection of data describing the Nation's forests, from plots located on a permanent grid.

FIA lichen gradient model—A quantitative model developed for a particular "FIA lichen model region." Such a model relates lichen community composition in the region to major environmental factors of interest, such as climate and air quality. Abbreviated after first use under a topic as "lichen gradient model," or just "model" in appropriate context and when usage is unambiguous.

FIA lichen indicator—Collectively refers to lichen species and communities as used in the standard national FIA Program as biomonitors of forest health, including all the different indexes developed from the lichen data collected, and more loosely to all aspects of lichens in the program. Often abbreviated in text as "lichen indicator."

FIA lichen indicator advisor—An FIA employee or contractor whose responsibility it is to advise and collaborate with the FIA Program on all aspects of the FIA lichen indicator from data collection through analysis and reporting to long-term planning. This person has a Ph.D. or equivalent professional training in both lichenology and community ecology. A major responsibility is to oversee maintenance of high standards related to lichenology expertise in all aspects of the program. Often abbreviated in text as "indicator advisor" or "lichen IA."

FIA lichen model region—A geographic area defined for the FIA Program for which a quantitative "FIA lichen gradient model" will link lichen community composition to major environmental factors of interest including climate and air quality. After such a gradient model has been developed, FIA plots within this region have response indexes calculated from lichen data for all environmental factors defined from the model for this region. Abbreviated after first use under a topic as "lichen model region" or just "region" in appropriate context and when usage is unambiguous.

FIA lichen plot—An almost-circular plot (gray area in fig. 4) with a 120-ft radius centered on FIA subplot 1, but excluding the area of the four subplots. Note that the lichen plot **does** overlap the area of the four large macroplots that are concentric with the four small subplots. Usually abbreviated as "lichen plot."

gradient—The term as used in plant ecology and for this document is defined as a range of values ordered from small to large (or vice versa) for either an environmental factor or a derived number representing some biotic factor of interest. For instance, an ordination axis score is a derived number that for a lichen gradient model represents an aspect of lichen species composition at one plot. The entire ordered range of scores for one ordination axis thus represents a species composition gradient. And the full ordered range of average summer high temperatures for a set of plots represents a gradient for summer temperature.

gradient length—The largest minus the smallest score on a published lichen model gradient (Will-Wolf and Neitlich 2010). Gradient length is reported in documentation for the lichen gradient model and does not change over time. Differences between resampled plots for lichen response indexes are converted to percentage of the published model gradient length for comparison with data quality objectives.

inventory—Defined for the FIA Program as a one-time assessment across a geographic region of the patterns of forest vegetation and its components based on field sampling of permanent plots.

inventory year—Defined for the FIA Program as the calendar year in which the majority of plots in that group were sampled: FIA database variable INVYR. A group of plots is identified each calendar year for sampling following standard program protocol, with most sampled during the spring through fall seasons of that year.

lichen air quality index—A unitless numerical index that represents the position of an FIA plot at one particular time on an air quality gradient defined from a quantitative "FIA lichen gradient model" for a particular "FIA lichen model region." This index is one of a class of derived "lichen response indexes." The index is calculated based on lichen species composition from one sample of a plot. The air quality gradient as defined is statistically independent of all other lichen response gradients defined for that particular lichen gradient model. The air quality gradient may be related to measured or modeled quantities of particular pollutants, but the index is not defined in terms of those measured units.

lichen climate index—A unitless numerical index that represents the position of an FIA plot at one particular time on a climate gradient defined from a quantitative "FIA lichen gradient model" for a particular "FIA lichen model region." This index is one of a class of derived "lichen response indexes." The index is calculated based on lichen species composition from one sample of a plot. The lichen climate gradient as defined is statistically independent of all other lichen response gradients defined for that particular lichen gradient model. The lichen climate gradient may be related to measured or modeled values of particular climate components such as average summer temperature or average annual rainfall, but the index is not defined in terms of those measured units.

lichen index—A unitless numerical value based on FIA lichen data that represents some defined relative response of lichens at an FIA plot. Both primary indexes and response indexes derived from a lichen gradient model are included under this phrase.

lichen response index—A unitless numerical value that represents the status of an FIA plot at one particular time with respect to one of the gradients defined for lichen response to an environmental factor from a quantitative lichen gradient model. The derived index is an indicator of lichen response to the environmental factor. Response index is calculated based on lichen species composition from one sample of a plot. Each lichen response gradient defined for a model is statistically independent of all other lichen response gradients defined for that particular model.

lichen species richness index—The count of macrolichen species recorded from an FIA plot surveyed following standard protocols. This primary index is available for any FIA plot surveyed for lichens; it is an indicator of relative (not absolute, see section "Plot-Level Attributes/Lichen species richness index," p. 21) diversity of the lichen community at that plot at that time. Often abbreviated after first use under a topic as "richness index" when usage is unambiguous.

measurement year—The year in which a plot was actually visited in the field for sampling: FIA database variable MEASYR. Most plots in an "inventory year" are visited for lichen sampling in the spring through fall seasons of the inventory year, but visits in the winter of the following year for lichen sampling are possible. In the latter case, measurement year and inventory year would differ.

monitoring—Defined for the FIA Program as repeated assessment over multiple years and across a geographic region of the patterns and trends of forest vegetation and its components from repeated field sampling of the same population of permanent plots.